Black Britain

A Critical Look at the Role of the
Media in Race Relations Today

Arrow

Arrow Books Limited
3 Fitzroy Square, London W1

An imprint of the Hutchinson Publishing Group

London Melbourne Sydney Auckland
Wellington Johannesburg and agencies
throughout the world

First published by Arrow Books Ltd 1975

Contents

6 *Contents*

Acknowledgements

I would like to thank Jean Goddard for the support and advice she continually provided whilst processing the manuscripts with her particular care and efficiency. Liz Husband, as wife of the editor, has fully earned all the usual clichéd thanks. As friend, as Liz, her contribution was unique. Thanks too to all the friends who have, usually unknowingly, contributed to the production of this book. Thanks to the readers who act upon it.

Introduction

This book emerged out of my involvement in a study of the impact of the British mass media upon the response of white Britons to the growing black population in Britain. That study* showed clearly the potent way in which the mass media did play a part in determining the white response to a black presence in Britain or 'coloured immigration' as it was more generally defined. The media were seen to both reflect and reinforce the prejudices and concerns of white Britain. In as much as the media influenced the response of white Britons to black individuals resident in Britain then the media were having an indirect impact upon the lives of black people resident in this society. And although it was not the concern of the study I was then involved in, it became very apparent that the British media also had more direct effects upon its black audience. The purpose of this book is to provide some insights into these various ways in which the British mass media impinge on the lives of black citizens of this society.

The contributions have been prepared by individuals who are both black and have experience of the British media; by white media professionals who as journalists have relevant experience in reporting race; and by academics, who are white and whose research has produced useful contributions to an understanding of the impact of the mass media in multiracial Britain. These people have provided a body of evidence and arguments which make it apparent that the relation of the mass media to the complex of experiences, beliefs and values

* Published as *Racism and the Mass Media*, by Paul Hartmann and Charles Husband, Davis-Poynter, London, 1974.

which shape the pattern of race relations in this country is not a tenuous link which merits only peripheral interest. On the contrary, through the variety of styles and over the range of areas examined there emerges a cumulative image of the considerable influence which the mass media exerts upon the feelings and beliefs of individuals, and hence upon race relations in Britain. Nor should this convergence of evidence be assumed to reflect the homogeneity of the authors. We are certainly not all known to each other, and I seriously doubt that we would all find each other congenial company for more than a limited time. Perhaps our only common characteristic is a commitment to justice and a desire to eradicate racism in all its forms.

As editor there are a few aspects of my interpretation of that role which are best shared at the outset. Since the issue of editorial censorship figures large in the experience of black and white when cooperating with the mass media, I foreswore any temptation to try and impose a common style, format or length on the contributions. This results in a great variation between articles which may for some be an irritant. There are statements which may stir resentment in the reader, but may I ask that before labelling the material offensive you first ask whether you are not being unquestioningly defensive. This book ought not to be a congenial read for anyone. Its purpose is not to provide definitive answers but to pose unpalatable but essential questions.

Throughout the book I have used the term 'black' to include all non-whites. This is not an accidental usage but represents a deliberate rejection of the alternative term 'coloured' which is associated with negative connotations. 'Black' has also been used because of its contemporary political connotations, for since racism is quintessentially a political reality it is appropriate to use a term which reflects the positive political consciousness of people who are rejecting an identity which has been imposed upon them and are now actively generating a positive black identity; one in which black is not only beautiful but also powerful.

The ordering of the contributions in the book is intended

to provide a minimal degree of continuity and a progression of arguments and evidence. In my contribution I have attempted to provide a brief introduction to the background of racism in this society and to point to the implications this has for the perception of mass media content. There follows a section composed of interviews with two people whose personal experience of the mass media provided immediate evidence of the inability of the media to meet the demands of black participants. The next section includes three contributions from academics who outline ways in which racist assumptions are embedded in entertainment and news media, and some of the implications of this are developed. This is followed by a section composed of contributions by working journalists whose different experiences present a different perspective on the same general area. Finally I have tried to provide some suggestions for action which may result in the creation of a more responsible mass media for multiracial Britain.

PART I

1. Racism in Society and The Mass Media: a critical interaction

Charles Husband

In Britain we have a variety of mass media operations which are dominated by white interest through ownership, staffing and the product they produce. This would not be a matter for concern were it not that also in Britain there is a significant black population whose labour is exploited, whose freedoms are curtailed and whose personal integrity is denigrated. In a modern industrial society like Britain the mass media play a significant part in sustaining the values and defining the immediate concerns of the society. The mass media provide a perspective from which we view our world and it is the fact that they provide a 'white' perspective for interpreting events in a *multiracial* Britain that demands our attention, and action. If the news media provide a definition of events in Britain in which the black population are presented as a threat whilst the realities of racial discrimination and the distribution of the vital social resources of housing, education, employment and welfare receive only superficial coverage, then we should not be complacent about the future welfare of what is already a multiracial society. Similarly if the entertainment media, television, radio, films, literature, are still dominated by an image of Britain as a white society where values which developed in a past era of imperial splendour still find easy expression ought we not to be concerned about the implications this must have for contemporary Britain? However, lest we focus too immediately upon the role of the mass media in this society it is helpful to pause to note that the mass media reflect the society within which they operate as well as influence that society. Therefore, before going on to examine the mass media in more detail let us first look at Britain and British culture as it relates to our multiracial present and future.

Britain is a nation with a long history of parliamentary rule; we pride ourselves on our legal system and on the freedom enjoyed by citizens of this country. Much of what the British think and feel now is pervaded by an appreciation of the long and glorious past. Nowhere is this more apparent than in the British self-perception of Britain as a tolerant society with a particular tolerance of immigrants, which is seen as a marked feature of our history. Yet this view of Britain's long established tolerance has acquired mythical properties not borne out by a closer examination of reality. In 1919 at a time when there was a considerable clamour against the entry of aliens into Britain, much of it anti-Semitic in nature, Josiah Wedgwood, MP, made a speech which has much contemporary relevance:

Generally speaking, aliens are always hated by the people of this country. Usually speaking, there has been a mob which has been opposed to them, but that mob has always had leaders in high places. The Flemings were persecuted and hunted, and the Lombards were hunted down by the London mob. Then it was the turn of the French Protestants. I think that the same feeling holds good on this subject today. You always have a mob of entirely uneducated people who will hunt down foreigners, and you will always have people who will make use of the passions of the mob in order to get their own ends politically.[1]

Less than two decades after Wedgwood's speech, Britain was again being offered an opportunity to demonstrate her tolerance toward immigrants. In 1938 the Jews in Nazi Germany were experiencing escalating hostility and violence from the regime there and after the pogrom of 'Crystal Night' their position was clearly desperate. The plight of the Jews was well recorded in the British press of the time and yet there was still considerable opposition to the unrestricted acceptance of Jewish refugees. So much so that a few days after the 'Crystal Night' pogrom the British Government announced plans to admit some 'selected' adults and a limited number of children for training prior to re-emigration to the colonies. It was felt that to do more would lead to a 'definite anti-Jewish movement in the country'.[2] This obscene manifestation of British concern for tolerance was also identified by Sharf in his study of this period:

... one basic assumption emerged, whether all its implications were consciously understood or not. If more Jewish refugees meant, or might eventually mean, more anti-Semitism in host countries, then the cause of anti-Semitism was – the Jew. And since anti-Semitism, at least in its more virulent form, was clearly wrong and barbarous, the only course was to prevent any notable increase in one's own Jewish population.[3]

The splendid casuistry of this formula lies in the way in which a stated concern for maintaining good relations between host society and immigrants can apparently justify an avoidance of responsibility and actual suppression of tolerant behaviour. It was a formula too good to be lost and as we shall see appears again.

More recently, in 1968, the shallowness of British tolerance was again clearly demonstrated in the popular uproar against the entry of East African Asians. In early 1968 the arrival of UK passport holders from East Africa had escalated massively following the dual pressures of Africanization in East Africa and fear amongst East Africans, following the campaigns of Enoch Powell and Duncan Sandys, that Britain was about to exclude them. These fears proved well founded when the Labour Government rushed through the 1968 Commonwealth Immigrants Act: an act specifically designed to discriminate against the entry of black individuals into Britain. Richard Crossman in an article in *The Times* (6 October 1972) provided an explanation of the Labour Cabinet's behaviour:

As progressives we were opposed to capital punishment, persecution of homosexuals and racial prejudice, whereas a large section of our working-class supporters regard such ideas as poison. What they hate most is our softness on colour. It nearly cost us the election of 1964 – particularly in the West Midlands – and it was widely felt that our improved majority of 1966 was due to our new tough line on immigration control. That is why as a Government we were panicked in the autumn of 1967 by top secret reports predicting a

mass expulsion of Asians from East Africa and began to make
contingency plans for legislation which we realized would have been
declared unconstitutional in any country with a written constitution
and a supreme court.[4]

In the 1960s and 70s it was not only Wedgwood's 'entirely
uneducated' or even Crossman's 'working-class supporters'
who were opposed to immigration but a progressively larger,
broadly based, consensus developed throughout all strata in
Britain which regarded further coloured immigration as
anathema and viewed the current coloured population as
representing a problem. Yet despite all the evidence to the
contrary we were still able to see ourselves as a tolerant nation.
In 1969 *Colour and Citizenship*,[5] a survey of race relations in
Britain, contained a study of 'the incidence of colour prejudice
in the white population' and this reported that only 10 per
cent of the population were 'prejudiced'. Indeed these findings
allowed the authors to conclude that, 'What is needed in short
is not an effort to make people unprejudiced, but rather to
remind them that they *are* unprejudiced.'[6] [Original emphasis.]
This conclusion was made despite the fact that in the same
study, of those people interviewed in the Nottingham sample,
when asked whether or not they considered the British, on
the whole, superior or inferior to the majority of people in
Europe, Asia, Africa and America: only 24 per cent regarded
the British as superior to the Americans, 38 per cent considered
them superior to Europeans, but 58 per cent considered the
British superior to Asians and 66 per cent regarded them as
superior to Africans.[7] The interpretation of the evidence in this
study has since received detailed criticism, but this occurred
within the pages of social science journals and not in the
national press where this 'evidence' of our national tolerance
received such eulogistic coverage.

Our concern for tolerance was once again being voiced in
1972 when Britain wrestled with the Ugandan Asian 'problem',
which revolved around our reluctance to accept our responsibility toward United Kingdom passport holders who were
being expelled from Amin's Uganda. Since the majority of
these refugees were of Asian stock we expressed our concern

in the well tried 1938 formula. There were those, of course, who were totally opposed to the admittance of any Ugandan Asians, and their sentiments were vociferously expressed in the *Daily Express* at the time. The more 'liberal minded', however, accepted that we had an obligation toward these people but were concerned at the implications of actually doing anything about it. It was an attitude typified by a *Times* leader of 14 August 1972 which argued that:

Immigrants already settled here stand to suffer more than anyone else from a rate of new immigration greater than the social body of the host country can digest, or than its prejudices can tolerate.

In other words, since as a tolerant nation we cannot condone any increase in racial prejudice, and since an increase in the black population would surely result in more prejudice, then we must resist any pressure to admit more blacks. In the event General Amin's racist intransigence made us more tolerant than we wished to be, but Mr Robert Carr made it clear that we could not endanger the welfare of 'those immigrants already resident here' by permitting any other East African country to similarly make us stand by our United Kingdom passport-holders. In January 1973 Mr Carr, the Home Secretary, said in a speech that:

When Asians resident in Uganda were summarily expelled last year the Government immediately accepted its obligations to our passport-holders who had nowhere else to go and the people of this country responded with characteristic generosity to the plight of the refugees.[8]

But the mass expulsion from Uganda and the necessity to cope with it has regrettably created a new situation. The Government considers that to have a similar burden thrust on us again would impose unacceptable strains and stresses in our society and not least would endanger our ability to carry out our duty to those immigrants already resident here.

The Government therefore thinks it right, at this time, when we have just swiftly and honourably accepted the Ugandan Asian refugees and when there is no threat to UK passport-holders elsewhere, to make it clear that while we shall continue to accept our responsibility to UK passport-holders by admitting them in a controlled and orderly manner through the special voucher scheme, this is as much as it is reasonable and realistic for us to do if good community relations are to be maintained in Britain.[9]

Thus with an exaggerated account of our 'honourable' behaviour toward the Ugandan Asians and with a reaffirmation of our commitment to the welfare of our immigrants Mr Carr in effect washes his hands of responsibility for the many Asian UK passport-holders still resident in East Africa.

Our record of tolerance is clearly not compatible with our self-image of ourselves as a liberal and tolerant nation. And yet, such is the strength of this belief in our tolerance that it inhibits any objective perception of our actual behaviour. Not only does this pathological acceptance of our national tolerance create an exaggerated estimation of 'tolerant' behaviour where it does occur, but more than this it makes any consideration that we may be positively intolerant well-nigh impossible. Very often prejudice is not seen where it exists, and where it is acknowledged it is perceived as a freak deviation from society as a whole. Thus we find a willingness to accept interpretations of racial prejudice which suggest that such prejudices are the product of the abnormal psychology of a minority of individuals. In this way responsiblity for such prejudice as is recognized can be detached from society as a whole and be attributed to a minority of social and psychological defectives who inevitably are found in every society. However, if we are going to understand the importance of the impact of mass media upon race relations in Britain today, then we must divest ourselves of the comforting myth of our national tolerance and painfully recognize that Britain is an endemically racist society.

Our response to the presence of black immigrants within our society has not been the consequence of our brief experience of the last twenty years or so. White resentment of a black population in this country has a long history and as long ago as Elizabethan England we were already heavily infected with colour prejudice. These were prejudices clearly well known to Shakespeare who could rely upon his audience's outrage at the thought of Desdemona being in the 'gross clasp of a lascivious Moor'. Indeed the strength of *Othello* was generated by the deliberate double-take which reversed the audience's expectations in giving black Othello the virtues usually associated with a white Christian. Nor was it only in the theatre that resentment was expressed toward blacks, for one consequence of Elizabethan involvement in the slave trade was the emergence of a significant black population in England. This black population aroused such resentment that Queen Elizabeth I deemed it necessary to proclaim that:

Whereas the Queen's majesty, tendering the good and welfare of her own natural subjects, greatly distressed in these hard times of dearth, is highly discontented to understand the great number of Negroes and blackamoors which (as she is informed) are carried into this realm . . . who are fostered and powered here, to the great annoyance of her own liege people that which covet the relief which these people consume, as also for that the most of them are infidels having no understanding of Christ or his Gospel: hath given a special commandment that the said kind of people shall be with all speed avoided and discharged out of this her majesty's realms.[10]

Even in the sixteenth century blacks were labelled as being a burden on the society and best suited to repatriation. This response was itself a natural expression of a culture which even then had for centuries possessed negative conceptions of blacks and blackness. For example Jordan[11] reports that the meaning of black before the sixteenth century included, 'Deeply stained with dirt; soiled, dirty, foul . . . Having dark or deadly purposes, malignant; pertaining to or involving death . . . iniquitous, atrocious, horrible, wicked. . . .' These were meanings which contributed to the description of the black person himself. Contact with the black cultures of West Africa only increased sixteenth- and seventeenth- century fascination with the 'exotic' blackman and served to generate new bizarre accounts of the inferiority of the black people. Indeed many of the early published accounts included much that was purely fanciful written alongside more realistic reports, which of course in themselves commented at length on the 'primitive' nature of the societies observed. It has been said that, 'by the eighteenth century a report on the sexual aggressiveness of African women was virtually required of European commentators'.[12] The same author suggests a commercial element in this interest for, 'of course, with many Englishmen actively participating in the slave trade, there were pressures making for descriptions of "hot constitution'd Ladies" possessed of a 'temper hot and lascivious, making no scruple to prostitute themselves to the Europeans for a very slender profit, so great is their inclination to white men.'[13] The sexual myths which emerged throughout British involvement in slavery are found today alive and well in racist jokes and beneath the surface in many 'polite' conversations.

Our commercial involvement in slavery also created a need for a system of beliefs which could justify such brutal and inhuman treatment of other human individuals as was carried out under chattel slavery. These justifications were built on existing beliefs and provided arguments which were claimed to demonstrate the inferiority of black races. First theological arguments, and then scientioc ones, were evolved to legitimate the slavery which was so profitable for our nation. The racist beliefs which were generated by our involvement in slavery metamorphosed into the racist paternalism of our 'great Empire'. The lineal descendants of these beliefs emerge in each generation, phoenix-like, from the ignorance and bitterness of people who are promised much and given little; from the guilty fears of the affluent; and from the self-interest of the powerful. Racism has a terrifying capacity for survival; born out of injustice and exploitation it feeds injustice and exploitation, and so guarantees its future environment.

In the survey already mentioned we found that still today 58 per cent of the sample are prepared to say that they consider the British superior to Asians and 66 per cent say the British are superior to Africans. It would be bad enough if as a nation we merely believed this but all the evidence is that we also act upon it. Recent research continues to demonstrate colour discrimination in employment[14] and the new-found militancy of the Asian labour force in the Midlands is making apparent the gross exploitation they suffer from employers and the neglect they receive from the 'white' trade unions,[15] which actively countenance the racial discrimination. In politics race has been an electoral gambit of the last decade with each new Immigration Act providing further official colour discrimination in response to the grassroots baying of the racist electorate. Typically, the official response toward increasing hostility toward the black population in Britain has been half-hearted and ineffective; the Race Relations Board, whose job it was to counter discrimination, has been shown to be slow, timid and totally lacking in real teeth. Similarly the Community Relations Commission has been a conservative, compromised body from its outset. A detailed study of community relations committees said in its conclusions that 'community relations committees, partly through their own choice, partly through the constraints of their position, tend to act as agencies of social control rather than social change'.[16] Convinced of our tolerance and continuing to perceive Britain as a white society that has black immigrants, rather than as a multiracial society with black and white citizens, we as a nation have sought to defend the old rather than adapt to the new. We are a society with racist beliefs entrenched in our culture and racial discrimination evident in our laws and in our behaviour. Because of this it is vital that when we look at the contents of the mass media and consider its impact upon white and black audiences we should remember the sort of society within which these media exist.

One feature of human behaviour makes it particularly relevant to constantly remember the racial hostility in our society, this feature being selective perception. Selective perception is the name social scientists give to that all too human foible of interpreting events or information in such a way as to suit our own desires and needs. Football matches are one venue where selective perception is frequently apparent; when your team's right back brings down the opposition forward it is a splendid solid tackle, but when the opposition defence brings down your forward it is a filthy foul and the referee is often given acid advice regarding his senility and dubious ancestry. At a more personal level it seems that many quarrels that would otherwise have died take on a new life when the combatants fall out anew over who started the argument in the first place. Selective perception is a ubiquitous, and it seems inevitable, part of human behaviour and it is found throughout the whole range of judgement situations. What people see is partially a consequence of the sort of people they are, of what their beliefs, fears, ambitions dispose them to expect and find more congenial. In the area of race relations recent research[17] has shown that in Britain people who were 'prejudiced' against black people tended to see the press as showing favouritism toward blacks, whilst people who were 'tolerant' saw the same press as being unfair toward them. An implication of this is that the 'prejudiced' people could infer that the blacks must be much more of a threat and problem than the press reported; whereas the 'tolerant' people could infer that blacks were not really such a problem as the press implied. Both groups of people were commenting on the same material and yet perceiving it very differently. It is evident that their interpretation of the press produced perceptions of events which were in both cases entirely consistent with their different pre-existing beliefs.

It is precisely because racist beliefs are so endemic amongst the white native population in Britain that we must anticipate a tendency for the content of the media to be interpreted in such a way so as to reinforce the existing prejudices. Also we may expect such racist assumptions and biases as occur within the content of the mass media to pass without comment from the majority of the white audience; since they share these assumptions they are likely to remain unnoticed; or if consciously identified they will be unobjectionable. Of course for a black audience these same assumptions may stand out in stark and bitter detail and be a source of anger and pain. However, since as we have noted the mass media are owned[18] and staffed by whites and their predominant audience is white, we must expect the complementary predominance of white values and assumptions within the mass media content. Let us briefly look at what sort of material the British mass media have offered up for interpretation through selective perception.

In the news media a study of the press reporting of race relations over the period 1963–70 provides some valuable evidence.[19] Over the period in question every thirteenth issue of *The Times*, the *Guardian*, the *Daily Express* and the *Daily Mirror* was examined and its contents analysed. The report of the content analysis says of the coverage of race relations over the period that:

. . . its main focus was on those aspects of the British situation that were central to political debate and action in regard to race and coloured people. Race in Britain was portrayed as being concerned mainly with immigration and the control of entry of coloured people to the country, with relations between white and coloured groups, discrimination and hostility between groups, with legislation, and with the politician, Enoch Powell, who has come to symbolise anti-immigrant feeling and concern about the number of coloureds in the country. These were the main terms in which race was presented, and when the subject of race appeared in the press, these themes were more likely to be evoked than others.[20]

The study showed that the press, through for example discussion of discrimination, had maintained the visibility of the official 'tolerant' values of British society, but that at the same time it had emphasized those features of the situation in which the black population was perceived as a threat and a problem. Since one of the journalist's responsibilities is to report what he observes in society, it is not perhaps surprising that much of the reporting reflected 'those aspects of the British situation that were central to political debate and action'.[19] However, we have already noted the pervasive racist underpinnings of much of the political debate, and consequent legislation, in the last decade and there was therefore a great need for journalists to fulfil another of their professional responsibilities which is not only to reflect events but to question and interpret them. The content analysis provides evidence that on the whole the press failed to carry out this function. For example, the study shows that as time passed, and hostility toward the black population and toward black immigration increased, so the press provided less discussion of the background to racial hostility, and the social conditions which foster it, and focused increasingly on the hostility itself, and its various manifestations. In other words there was little analysis of the relation of the black population to the social resources of housing, education and employment, where so often the black population were the scapegoats wrongly blamed for the national deficiencies in the provision of these resources. There was even less comment about the positive contribution the black population made to the economy and to the society, for which there was ample evidence. In retrospect it was apparent that the press had reflected the hostility, had accepted the definitions which focused upon the black population as a problem and had projected an image of Britain as a white society in which the black population was an aberration.

In as much as conflict is a staple ingredient of newscopy it is perhaps only natural that press coverage of race relations should be heavily pervaded by conflict, with a natural emphasis on the problematic. In fact there was evidence of the homogenizing effect of normal journalistic procedures in that the study showed a considerable similarity between the four papers in their coverage of race. There were of course different editorial attitudes on the issues reported but great similarity in the definition of what were the issues and the relative importance which should be attached to them. For example, over the period the four papers may have had differing views about it, but they did agree that black immigration was a problem and that it should be 'curbed'. This news consensus has important implications for it suggests that the bulk of the white population will have little opportunity for encountering any alternative ways of defining national events and interpreting them. The probability must have been, and still must be, that the majority of the white audience receiving news media definitions of events would find a statement that black immigration is a threat and a problem quite reasonable. Or put another way, few would respond to such a statement with the question 'Why?' Throughout the period of increasing hostility toward immigration there has been a general acceptance that immigrants are black and a refusal to acknowledge, or consider, that black people are only a part of the total immigration. Throughout the era of the 'numbers game' it became a ritual enacted on a repetitive basis for Mr Powell to produce a projected figure of the future black population in Britain and for 'liberal' commentators to dispute his statistics. What was not disputed was his assumption that a large black population was in some way an evil to be avoided. Faced with the frequently repeated statement that black immigration is a threat and a problem, the press, the race pundits and the audience, have not asked – 'Why is this so?' It has been an apparent truth that was beyond doubt; it conjured forth emotions and beliefs in the white audience which made it an impossible question to ask, for the answer would be literally incredible. Why is black immigration a threat and a problem – because of white racism. No wonder the question was not asked.

It was a question which a responsible news media should have asked and forced upon us. However, the news media have reported race relations in too uncritical a way; they have reflected racist assumptions and reported without adequate analysis racist behaviour and racist policy. Perhaps it is unreasonable to expect white journalists operating in white-owned enterprises to do better than their audience. Yet recent research[21] has indicated that the news media do have a significant impact upon how white Britons perceive race relations in this country and for that reason we must be very concerned that the content of the news media has provided definitions of events which have reflected racism rather than challenged it. For a white audience this is tragic in that it must tend to reinforce their existing prejudices, but what of the black audience?

To be a black resident of this country is to be subject to a continuous assault on your identity and integrity. Your presence in this country is signalled to you as being unreal since the news media refuse to see you as a citizen, but as an immigrant. Your own identity based on family connections with a specific island community is seldom acknowledged since at best you are described as West Indian, or for those with links to specific small communities in India, Pakistan or Bangladesh the important variations in culture and religion are lost under the label of Asian. The possible arrival of more people with a similar background to yourself is reported in the press in the language of natural disasters as 'a flood' or 'tidal wave'. A continuing assumption implicit in much of the news programming is that in various ways you and your kind are an unwanted burden, a black parasite on a white society. The 'whiteness' of the society you have joined is made apparent in the concern expressed regarding your undesirable propensity for breeding more like yourself to further dilute the national identity. These aspects of news have made it difficult for black citizens of this country to feel accepted and settled here. Indeed, it is more accurate to say that they are 'tolerated'; tolerated as something essentially unpleasant which must be put up with.

The black audience of the British news media has also seen the concern for equality and tolerance which has been apparent in the news media but for many of them it has been perceived with bitterness and irony. When concern for you is expressed in terms of keeping people of your colour and background out of the country then tolerance takes on a perverted appearance. When legislation enacted in the name of equality visibly fails to defend your rights and yet is not seriously challenged in the news media you feel that these media must belong to someone else. When at a local level you know of blacks fighting against exploitation and harassment and see the press presenting a biased truth, a white truth, then you know to whom the media belong. For if exploitation of black workers in South Africa can become a front-page issue, then it is reasonable for black workers here, with their personal knowledge of events, to draw their own conclusions from the news media's neglect of exploitation within Britain. It would need little help from selective perception for black citizens of Britain to conclude that they are the forgotten audience of a hostile medium. Like children before autocratic parents they may hear themselves discussed but on no account join in the conversation. As Wilfred Wood points out, there can be severe penalties exacted through misquotation and selective editing threatening the credibility of any black who is brash enough to join that conversation.

It can hardly be surprising therefore if many in the black community are highly suspicious of the British news media and the motives of its personnel. For many blacks the content of the news media may be personally threatening and for others it will reinforce their decision to maintain only minimal, and largely economic, contact with a society that so visibly rejects them. If the news media provide an interpretation of events which reinforce the prejudices of the white audience, it is likely that they reinforce the experience of the majority of the black audience. For, in their daily life they are treated as inferior and alien and the news media, through their neglect of the concerns of their black audience, present a white view of an essentially white society and thus reflect the sentiments underlying the hostility and discrimination which the black audience experiences.

What of the entertainments media, what material do they provide to their audience for selective interpretation? Let us consider television which represents a source of entertainment and which has a large and regular audience. One thing that is immediately apparent about entertainment on television is the relative absence of black people. A recent study by Equity Coloured Artists' Committee[22] showed that, in the programmes they watched in the week Sunday 26 May until Saturday 1 June 1974, out of a total of 891 artists seen on all three channels during the week, only forty-five were coloured, and twelve of these were members of the Harlem Globetrotters team. Also no coloured artist played a leading role in any drama programme or comedy series, and there were only four supporting roles played by coloured artists in these programmes. These findings are entirely consistent with previous studies of television content[23] and indicate the way in which white ownership and control reflects itself in white content. It is not of course merely the absolute number of appearances of black actors in drama and comedy series which is important, but also the fact that so seldom do they have anything other than a minor supporting role or walk-on parts. One consequence of this is that in the world of television entertainment black people tend to be always the subordinates, those who follow but never command. Often they are no more than stage dressing for the actions of the white protagonists. In a fairly obvious way there is a similarity between the world of television entertainment and the reality of life in Britain today, black people do tend to be in inferior occupations, to occupy inferior housing, and to be subject to decisions made on their behalf by a white elite. Yet as we have noted the situation in Britain today arises from the racism in this society and for television entertainment to present a similar world is to reinforce the racism of the white audience. In fact television entertainment frequently fails to reflect British multiracialism where it exists. As the Equity report pointed out, black people had been markedly under-represented in programmes like *Crossroads, Coronation Street* and *General Hospital* where the supposed location for these 'soap operas' should normally have a significant black population. In fact since a large proportion of the blacks in television entertainment occur in imported American programmes the television drama portrayal of Britain shows it to be nearly as white as many racists who bay for repatriation would wish.

Even where black people occupy visible and significant parts in drama they can be portrayed in particularly unfortunate roles. For example, in the past few years when the news media have generated a paranoid concern over illegal immigration [of blacks of course] this spurious problem has emerged in at least three popular drama series. *The Saint, Softly Softly* and *The Strange Report* all had an episode centring on the illegal entry of blacks into Britain. Thus an issue which resonated perfectly with all the most deeply hidden chauvinist and racial fears of the white audience was given further credence by dramatic elaboration. Elaboration which in the case of one of these programmes resulted in the illegal immigrants being portrayed as the cause of a smallpox scare; with resulting scenes of old people and children trudging to the mobile clinic to receive their immunization.

4. Quoted in Derek Humphry and Michael Ward, *Passports and Politics,* Penguin Special, 1974, p. 89.

5. E. J. B. Rose and associates, *Colour and Citizenship,* Institute of Race Relations/Oxford University Press, London, 1969.

6. ibid, p. 737.

7. Quoted in: Daniel Lawrence, *Black Migrants: White Natives,* Cambridge University Press, London, 1974, p. 62.

8. See Humphry and Ward, *Passports and Politics,* for an alternative account of the events at that time.

9. Quoted in Humphry and Ward, *Passports and Politics,* p. 144.

10. Quoted in: James Wolvin, *The Black Presence,* Orbach and Chambers, London, 1971, p. 64.

11. Winthrop D. Jordan, *White Man's Burden,* Oxford University Press, 1971, p. 6.

12. ibid. p. 19.

13. ibid. p. 19.

14. See for example the P.E.P. reports: David J. Smith, *Racial Disadvantages in Employment,* P.E.P., London, 1974, and *The Extent of Racial Discrimination,* P.E.P., London, 1974.

15. See for example: *The Report of a Committee of Inquiry into a dispute between employees of the Mansfield Hosiery Mills Limited, Loughborough, and their employer,* H.M.S.O., London, 1972, which despite its evasion of the racism present in the situation, provides an interesting version of what was a very catalytic resistance by Asian workers to the coalition of white union leadership and employer. See also: 'Black People and Trade Unions' in *Race Today,* August, 1973, pp. 235–246.

16. Michael J. Hill and Ruth M. Issacharoff, *Community Action and Race Relations,* Institute of Race Relations/Oxford University Press, London, 1971, p. 203.

17. Paul Hartmann and Charles Husband, *Racism and the Mass Media,* Davis-Poynter, London, 1974, p. 93.

18. For a useful discussion of the control and ownership of the mass media see: Graham Murdock and Peter Golding, 'For a Political Economy of Mass Communications' in *The Socialist Register 1973,* eds, Ralph Miliband and John Saville, The Merlin Press, London, 1974, pp. 205–234.

19. Paul Hartmann, Charles Husband and Jean Clark, 'Race as News' in J. D. Halloran (ed), *Race as News,* UNESCO, 1974: and in precis form in: Paul Hartmann and Charles Husband, *Racism and the Mass Media,* Chapter 7.

20. Hartmann and Husband, ibid., p. 144.

21. Hartmann and Husband, *Racism and the Mass Media.*

22. British Actors' Equity Association, *Coloured Artists on British Television.* A Report produced by the Equity Coloured Artists' Committee, London, 1974.

23. For example, Bradley S. Greenberg, *Non-Whites on British Television*, BBC Audience Research Department, London, 1972: and in Hartmann and Husband, p. 199.

24. For a more extended discussion of the significance of films shown on television see Hartmann and Husband, pp. 189–95.

25. In a brief account such as this it has not been possible to describe the constraints of production which inevitably impinge on the opportunity for reflection and considered decision making in the news media. Similarly there has been no discussion of the way in which the very professionalism of the journalist often is in conflict with the needs for considered in depth treatment of race relations situations. These issues are developed in Hartmann and Husband, Chapter 8.

PART II

The two contributions in this section are statements generated by the personal experience of two people who in their different ways have encountered the white media. Wilfred Wood was born in Barbados and has lived in Britain since 1962. He has been closely involved in the development of black self-help projects. He was for a time Chairman of the Institute of Race Relations and is currently Chairman of the Martin Luther King Foundation and a member of the British Broadcasting Corporation's Religious Advisory Committee. Through his long involvement in race relations at grassroots level in London and by his significant contribution to organizations directly involved in countering racism he has acquired the respect of many in the black community. Because of this he has also been identified by the mass media as a potential 'spokesman' for black interests and has thus through his encounters with the news media added to his expert knowledge of the various manifestations of racial bias and ignorance; including the bias found in television journalism.

Yulisa Amadu Maddy was born in Sierra Leone and is best known in Britain as a playwright and author; for example *Obasai and Other Plays* and *No Past No Present No Future*, both in the Heinemann African Writers Series. He has been Head of Drama on Radio Sierra Leone, director of ZADACO and trainer of the National Dance Troupe in Zambia and has worked in the media in Britain and Denmark. It is his work in drama which has brought him face to face with the cultural conceits and racial bias of British theatre, both on the stage and in the mass media.

These are two very different people and, though their contact with the mass media has occurred in different capacities with different branches of the media, there are very significant similarities in what they are saying. Though in different ways their appeal to the media stems from their unique expertise as representatives of black opinion or black art, they are proscribed in the limitations imposed upon their freedom to express alternative values. They must take part on the terms of the media professionals, accept their white conceptions of events, yield to their definition of art, or not take part at all. Running as a theme through the comments of Wilfred Wood and Amadu Maddy is the unembarrassed domination of white values in the media. Blackness for the media is a physical characteristic not an outlook on life and if blacks are to appear in the media they must remain black vessels carrying white cargo.

2. Black Voices in the Media: an interview

Reverend Wilfred Wood

C.H. Wilfred Wood, for some years now you have been closely involved in the activities of black communities in Britain, and one consequence of your involvement has been the way in which the mass media have sought to use you as a ready source of comment on the race relations situation. I wonder if you could tell me of some of your experiences with the mass media.

W.W. It just occurred to me that there were three specific instances which might be of interest – two minuses and one plus you might say. The minuses: I remember when the extension of the Race Relations Act was being introduced in Parliament by the Labour Government – I think it was Mr Callaghan – I got a telephone call from *News at Ten* – Richard Linley was reporting for them – and he said he was interested in my coming on *News at Ten* – an interview for *News at Ten* – and could he come along and speak to me about the Race Relations Act. So I said, 'Yes, by all means.' He came to my house with a prepared set of questions and a prepared view of the Race Relations Act and the things that should be taken up with it. I listened to him and said, 'But much of this is really irrelevant.' He said, 'But you see, the Home Secretary's going to be saying so-and-so and so-and-so and we would like you to say so-and-so and so-and-so.' I said, 'No, that's really quite irrelevant – I'm not really interested in saying that – I'll tell you what the situation is as I see it, as someone who has followed the development up to this point.' So we had a good long talk and then he said, 'Well, my researchers are out interviewing people and so on, and if we need you I'll get in touch with you.' And I said, 'Fine, OK.' As soon as he stepped out of the door, in fact, I think I still had the door open to see him off, the telephone rang and that was the BBC *24 Hours* – and could I come on that programme this evening about the Race Relations Act, so I said, 'Look, what are you planning to do?' They said, 'The thing is, we are going to have one Conservative MP who agrees with it and one Conservative MP who's opposed to it, and we're going to have one Labour MP who's for it and one Labour MP who's against it, and we're going to have a black militant spokesman, Obe Egbuna, and we thought that you as a moderate person would be very good. We'd like you to come and put your moderate line.' So I said, 'I'm not interested in coming and putting any moderate line, and in any case how much do you think a chap would be able to say on a programme that's probably going to last about nine minutes, if they have so many people on. I tell you what, I'll come under these conditions – that you invite Vishnu Sharma to put the view from the Indian side.' – Oh yes, they were also going to have an Indian and a Pakistani and a West Indian.

C.H.   Everybody balanced out?

W.W.   Yes, but if you invite Vishnu Sharma who's an Indian, and if you invite Jeff Crawford who's a West Indian, I'll come along on the specific understanding that you put a single question to each of us, and not at all three of us to argue among ourselves about the same question, because each of us has a specialist knowledge in a particular field. Vishnu can talk about what happens at a Port of Entry and what the restrictions mean in terms of human beings and so on. And Crawford can talk in terms of the representations made by the immigrant organizations about the Act, and I can speak in terms of what the local community relations councils tried to do or should have been doing and didn't do. So, needless to say, they said, 'Well, thank you very much but we'll call you again if we think it's necessary', and, needless to say, neither of them called me again.

Another good example is, I got a call from a girl who's working on the Frost programme and she said, 'Well, we think that these various people, race relations and so on, have all got it wrong, and we're going to do a Frost programme on race and we'd like you to take part.' So I said, 'Can you tell me what you plan to do?' I listened a bit to what they planned to do – I can't really remember except that it was pretty awful. I said, 'If you really want to make any contribution to race relations, the best thing you could do is not to do that, but since this is going to be the last programme in the series anyway, spend the time between now and the next series doing some proper research and do a really good programme in the Frost series when it comes back.' So she said, 'Well, we are still thinking about it – thank you very much indeed, if we need to get in touch with you again we will.' And in fact they didn't put the programme on but it is significant that they had instead a hotch-potch about Joan Littlewood's theatre workshop and things like that. What it really amounted to was it was the last one in the series and they had nothing to fill it with and if you have nothing to fill it with you then turn to blacks and coloureds and so on, and in principle you can always find a sufficient number of blacks who are only too glad to get on television.

C.H. Was that the Frost programme which caused a good deal of disquiet because of the way in which the discussion was carried out?

W.W. No, this approach was some time ago – all right? Now you come to the last Frost programme, the one which they did in fact do. I got a telephone call from the Frost programme – they said they'd been talking to various people about doing this all-black Frost programme and everyone says that I should be invited to come on, so I said, as usual, 'What are you planning to do?' They said, 'Well, we're going to have all the people in the studio black'. I said, 'How many will that be then?' 'About 180 to 200'. I said, 'How are you going to get all those black people?' and she said, 'Well, that is a bit of a problem but we'll probably have to issue block invitations – will you come? You will, of course, be treated as a specialist.' I said, 'I don't think I'll come if you don't mind, but ring me again tomorrow.' It so happened that I was at that time meeting with a number of black colleagues who are all involved in different things and I had a quick word with them. I phoned back and said that some friends and I, all of whom are black people, that, if the programme is to be any good, we really should be on the programme and we have decided that we will come on the programme provided one of us takes over from David Frost. So the chap thought at first I was joking – 'I mean, you know, as it is, Mr Frost is going to be the only white person in the studio.' I said, 'Well precisely! Why should he be the only white person if it is a programme about black people? I'm telling you these people I know are more capable of drawing out from these black people a very constructive discussion and debate than Mr Frost is.' He said, 'Well, you know, Mr Frost is quite an expert in this field – how do you expect to compete? I don't think you have anyone of that calibre.' I said 'Now, how do you know that we have no one – have you ever seen any black person doing this, and what is more there was a time when nobody knew your Mr Frost – he had to start sometime – so why can't a black person do it?' This went on for a little time and then he got angry and said, 'Are you saying that the only time you and your friends will come on this programme is if one of you takes over from Mr Frost?' I said, 'That is precisely the case, yes.' All right, thank you very much, and I put the receiver down and that was the end of that. I still believe quite frankly that every black person who appeared on that programme should be fined because a number of them are intelligent enough to know that it was bound to end as it did, and I blame all of them, frankly – I don't know if you saw the programme. But anyone who goes round to West Indian meetings and so on knows that if you issue block invitations for the most part you have to issue them to organizations. If a person is in an organization, and he's the kind who gets an invitation, if he's one of the officers or an activist or something, he can't go along to a programme and just sit there. The very fact that he belongs to an organization means he's some kind of activist – he has something to say – and people from his group, or his acquaintances, will be expecting to hear him say something on the programme because he was on it. So the 180 people who were brought in to form the audience were not good audience material – they were talkers and actors and so on – that's the first thing. The second thing is that, frankly, quite often at West Indian meetings, West Indians may know how to start talking and to make their points and so on but unless you are very good you never get them to stop talking – they go on and on and on. So sometimes I have seen this situation – when a chap keeps talking and it's almost with a sigh of relief that he sits down when he's interrupted by somebody else because he doesn't know how to bring his remarks to a close. So what happens then is that there is a system whereby a chap is interrupted; sooner or later someone interrupts too early as time begins to run out and you then have a slanging match because he hasn't finished what he's saying. It's therefore the easiest thing in the world for a man who's conducting a discussion, like David Frost, if he gets into trouble to pick on an individual in the audience or to make fun of him or to encourage two groups in the audience to row rather than concentrate on the issue – that's normal. In fact, this was perfectly illustrated in the Frost programme in that at one stage the group there was showing a kind of unanimity and Frost, knowing that this wasn't what he had in mind then said to them, 'We know that you have differences among yourselves, there's no need to have a spurious agreement – what do you think of President Amin?' You see, knowing that he's got some Asians and some West Indians and that if there's one issue to bring out it's President Amin – he introduced President Amin at that stage because he's worried about this apparently solid front. Now another thing is that when they organize programmes like this they will come and put on the front row or in places near the microphones certain people that they consider important. Since for the most part these people they consider important are made important not by black communities – they aren't elected leaders of any kind – they are made important because they are accessible to the media or something like that. What happens is that you parade these people in the front row and you already have their names, their names will come up on the monitor when they are speaking, and he turns to them and says, 'Mr So and So, you are of such an importance, what do you think?' and you build up tremendous resentment from the other black people in the back who object to these chaps, who as far as they are concerned never do anything or are nuisances. Therefore you have a spectacle again of a collection of black people rowing and shouting at each other. Anyone who knows anything about these programmes or anything about black people knows that it was absolutely inevitable that the Frost programme would end as it did. I've seen it happen so many times – that's why I refused invitations on the Muggeridge Show, when again they were trying to treat the same questions in precisely the same way and Muggeridge holding forth for a long time – then some kind of foreign expert and then about fifteen or sixteen people were given three minutes in which all of these people who were also hand-picked as activists or something, having a slanging, shouting match. That's what they're always doing whenever you see them – they're shouting at each other and so on, so that you have all these people who are made black leaders and black spokesmen because they are accessible. I think that is one of the reasons why intelligent people in black communities shun any suggestion of leadership roles because they don't come up from below – they are appointed by the media.

C.H. I suppose one of the implications of what you're saying is that if you see a black spokesman on the mass media it's quite likely that he represents nobody but himself because those who do wouldn't go on that sort of programme?

W.W. That is the case. More and more of us now have decided, as it were, that this is not our scene, and really good people in the black community, doing solid work for the black community, avoid the television. Now what I've just said applies to so many television programmes, certainly the ones that I've refused to take part in. I make one exception, and that is the team that has just done that *Panorama* programme on Monday – 'Listen Man' it was called with Alan Hart and Michael Starks. As a result of this programme, I have quite some considerable respect for that particular team. I'll tell you what's in that programme apart from the rest – that when they started to research in much the same sort of superficial way as the others, they discovered that they didn't know very much about it. They were absolutely hounded by all the usual self-made spokesmen of the black community who wanted to get on the box, who wanted to shout whatever their particular lines are, and they did go through the motions and they did film most of these fellows in fact. Now they pleaded with me to come on the programme because they weren't short of material and they weren't short of stuff to portray what most white people believe. In other words with the amount of stuff that they had, if they had wanted to produce the same kind of programme which reinforces all the white stereotypes of blacks it could easily have been done because these black chaps were only too anxious to say all the things they thought would appeal to white people, and to be fair to them, they avoided this kind of thing. If they wanted to pander to that image they could easily have done it, and I think that, on the contrary, they considered themselves to be attempting to educate quite an ignorant white opinion. For example, some of the questions that he put were questions which he knew the answers to because we'd gone through them, but quite rightly I think he was saying that, 'If I, a comparatively intelligent person of some responsibility, was so far wrong about this I know that the vast majority of people out there are like this. Therefore, I will ask this question although it is going to sound stupid, and do answer it however you want and if necessary tell me off.' So I would rate the work that went into that, and the intentions, better than the average. I think on the average really they're doing a programme and this is what people generally believe and they don't educate themselves any more – when they've done it, they've done it – they go on to do something else – and I think this was the difference. This particular team may well have made enemies for themselves because as I said a lot of the black self-made spokesmen were turned down, and a number of them were actually filmed but edited out.

C.H.   Do you think that the mass media have a specific need for black spokesmen they can rely on to come forward at any time?

W.W.   Well yes, I think they have, without a doubt. You see, there may be a few good, well-researched long-term programmes where, even so, I suspect that unless you have a name it is difficult to get the money and the talent to do it properly. But this instant news thing, fitted into a slot, has a tremendous devouring capacity and therefore you want someone who is at the end of a telephone. You want someone that you can nip out and get an interview with because this thing has broken today and it's going to be on this evening, and possibly you want someone who is good television. What, ideally, you want as far as the black community is concerned is someone like the black equivalent of Clive Jenkins. Again Jenkins is good television – whatever he has to say – however alarmist – is generally well researched in the sense that he can back it up. If there was such a black spokesman who was sufficiently powerful *to command the terms* under which he appears on the box, this would counter some of the vulnerability of the black community, in terms of the way the media 'use' black spokesmen. You see, I did break my own rules, for example, to take part in that particular programme because I always said that I wouldn't go on anything that wasn't live, so that what I say is what I say. There's no recording – you're not going to edit out what I had to say and then I have to spend the rest of my day going round talking to black viewers saying, 'Well, I didn't actually say that – you picked it up half-way through – what I had said was. . . .' This tends to happen because nearly always white reporters ask the wrong questions – you have to say to them, 'No, you're wrong about so and so, that's not true, your premise is wrong, we don't really believe that.' Things like that – and no reporter likes having to be corrected all the time.

C.H.   This means you have to try to redefine the basis of the discussion, while at the same time the interviewer, through the questions he uses, is trying to impose his assumptions upon you.

W.W.   Exactly what *he* had in mind. I remember even in this one when we were talking, Al Hart, referring to what he thought was the new mood among blacks as a result of Malcolm X and the magazines and so on said, 'It is true, isn't it, that until Malcolm X and so on blacks did think of themselves as inferior – this black consciousness is a good thing for them?' I said, 'That's the kind of thing white people believe, but I have never met any black man who believed himself inferior – I've just never met one – I grew up among them and I've never met any single black man who believed himself inferior. If you look at the Caribbean literature or African literature, or the folk stories or the verbal traditions, the old traditions, you always see that in these the black man, despite the fact that he's at a disadvantage in that he hasn't got the money or he hasn't got the means of controlling power, he's always shown to outsmart, to outwit, the white man who has these things. No black chap believes he's inferior – what they confuse the situation with is that, just as in South Africa, black people don't go attacking machine guns with bare fists and so on because that would be stupid – it doesn't mean that you accept the superiority of white people. You devise means whereby you get around the situation because life must go on and you work your way in and out of the system, and you don't accept it as being any law of God. What happens is that black adults who to some extent have had this kind of experience seem to be comparatively cautious compared with young blacks who haven't had that kind of experience, but this consciousness of the young, is it a new thing which their fathers didn't have?

C.H.   What do you foresee for the future in terms of the role of the mass media and its effects on the black community in particular, and through that its effects on race relations in Britain?

W.W.   I think on the whole we will find the black community contracting out of it and therefore it is going to be very dangerous for the simple reason that the only people that you'll find talking to them are the people who are bound to mislead. The strength of the black community will be growing and be developing out of reach as it were and will not be covered by the mass media. I think if you can check with the *Panorama* people they will testify to this, because this is about the third time that they attempted to do a programme and this is the only one that got any measure of co-operation, after they had been dragged through the dust in a way before anyone would even talk to them. So I think that what will happen is that, as more and more black groups get hold of things, they see equipment and video-tape and so on, they'll be producing and making their own teaching films and so on with which they can educate black groups up and down the country – which will be out of reach of the mass media and I think this is already developing.

C.H.   You mean that in the future what will happen is that the white population will know progressively less and less?

W.W.   Yes, I think so, and you see if you want to avoid this you will have to do something more about getting black people, and I don't mean Uncle Toms, involved in news presentation and as part of the production teams that do current affairs and so on. Because you need some personnel who can provide a black perspective on events. This is in the interests of the white society, not even a black society, because in a way the black society will develop regardless, and develop away from white society, and if the mass media want to serve the whites they will have to think in terms of having blacks and not just merely up front but in the production areas of this kind of thing.

C.H.   Because otherwise the mass media will continue

reporting the symptoms and failing to attack the causes of the disease?

W.W.   Oh yes. The mass media is discredited with the black community, but they have no means of knowing that they are discredited with the black community because they have no contact. If they want to go on feeding the ignorance of the whites, they're welcome to do so, but it wouldn't really be doing anything to improve their standing with the blacks. Which may be a good thing because it is a fact that sometimes you have spasmodic goodness and erratic goodness confusing the issue, and you're better off sometimes when they are all jolly bad – it relieves you of having to continue discriminating and distinguishing between the whole lot of them.

'if involve B's 'its
beneficial both 2 B + W +
B's will develop away
from Mainstream anyway
+ if Media wants to
improve their standing
with B's must include
them

3. Creating a Black Theatre in Britain: an interview

Yulisa Amadu Maddy

C.H. Probably the best thing is if you start off by giving us a background to your qualifications for talking here – what you've done as an author, as a playwright and as an actor.

A.M. My only qualification for talking here is that I am a very stubborn, uncompromising, blackman. A blackman who finds himself hemmed in by a white Christian society that refuses to recognize certain obvious realities:

(a) that a human being is a human being regardless of pigmentation, race and colour; (b) that despite the many biased/unbiased race codifications, classifications and specifications based on scientific researches and psychological analyses, a man is a man, is another human being and is equal to any other man; (c) that any nation that at one time or other lived and prospered on the wealth of other nations, thrived on the labour of other nations, encouraged and welcomed immigrants for no other reason than to have cheap labour – another form of slavery – must be prepared to come to terms with the exploited.

In short my qualification is not a degree or a diploma gained from one of those fine institutions in a civilized developed Britain. My qualification is merely that I am one of the sons of the underdeveloped countries. One of those who will always refuse to be exploited. To be used. To be given a condescending pat or nod or smile.

I have qualified myself to fight the wrongs that are shamelessly practised and perpetrated in this civilized limbo of hypocritical dogooders who never mean what they say or do what they mean.

But, let me also make it quite clear that I do not belong nor do I subscribe to glib loud-mouth political awareness that has overtaken street niggers, Uncle Toms and licking-arse blacks who go around Britain shouting 'Black is Beautiful', 'Peace and Love', etc.

I don't have to eat 'Soulfood' to identify with soul-brothers and soul-sisters. I have no time to go about trumpeting 'Peace and Love' when all about and around me is war.

If there is enough time I will come back to this question of being a blackman in my own way and not identifying with the street nigger blackman.

As a playwright/actor I contributed a great deal to the making of the BBC African theatre in the early sixties. I wrote and acted in a considerable number of plays until I left to work in Denmark. Then it was quite a challenge because I was just starting to write and act. I was naive and very humble, accepting or rather taking everything for granted. The BBC African service was like a springboard. Some of the producers were quite likeable and genuine, come to think of it. Others were just plain English. Like the weather. However, I don't hang around there any more because now I know better and I detest most of the programmes they 'can' for African Radio stations. I detest them because they are immature and lacking in standard and calibre. But, if the African governments can go on accepting them I cannot stop them.

The BBC African service aside, I worked in Denmark for three-and-a-half years freelancing for the Danish Radio and Newspapers. I also introduced and ran an African theatre there until 1968 when I went back to Sierra Leone. In 1969, I went to Lusaka, Zambia, on a two-year contract with TBM Publishing Enterprises. While in Zambia I was seconded to the Ministry of Culture as Adviser and Trainer of the Zambian National Dance Troupe.

On returning to London I worked as Head of Drama for the Keskidee Centre in Islington. Here for the first time I was confronted with the horrible loss of cultural identity common among black youths born in Britain and those who had come to live here at a very early age.

Unable to do my work as I think fit for the good of these kids, I was tactfully forced to resign, which I did.

Since August of 1973 I started my own theatre company – Gbakanda theatre – and from time to time am contracted to direct professional companies. One of them being the 'Dark and Light Theatre' which is in my opinion the only serious happening so far as theatre for and among black people in Britain is concerned.

C.H. When you started writing did you start off as someone who had something to say – do you have a motivation behind writing or is it just a fascination for writing?

A.M. I write because I can make a job of it, just like a cobbler can be a good craftsman or just a cobbler.

I am not interested in the novelties and greatness of 'The Writer' or 'The Artist'. I am a man who wants to contribute genuinely to my people – Sierra Leoneans – first and foremost – something which is very much lacking: a written literature of Sierra Leone; about Sierra Leoneans.

I could have become a lawyer if I thought I had the gift and talent.

I know my limitations. For me writing is as good a job as any. Whether I will ever make a decent living out of it is another question since the white world controls what is to be published and who and when.

Anyhow, I consider myself very lucky, lucky in the sense that my first three plays were accepted and produced by the BBC Radio. Then another play was done on TV and so it goes on. To date I have three books to my name and am published in quite a few anthologies.

As to having something to say as a writer, I don't preach. What the facts are, the faults, the mistakes, the truths and the problems that make us human in my part of the world are all there in black and white. Some like it, some hate it. So I think I am saying something.

C.H. Have you evolved to someone who is aware of any particular political position or did you start off with a political position?

A.M. My politics is to see that justice is done not just talked about by those who 'know best' how to rule others.

Until I was thirty years old I never really felt any real urge to think seriously of practical politics. I was among the suffering millions who go through life mushroom headed, indifferent and naive even to their own interests and rights. You might say that I was a brainwashed child accepting and believing that others – whiteyman – knows best what was good for me.

You can imagine my hate for all whites when to my horror I discovered that all through my life I was not even considered a human object by the people whom I was brought up to love, respect and obey.

It took me thirty years to wake up from the drugged nostalgia and become an aggressive, uncompromising savage political animal.

Politically I have not done my own thing yet. I have denounced a lot of the 'isms' and claptrap of both East and West. I will, given time and left alone, evolve to someone who is very well aware of his particular political position. When I do it will be something else and something new. For the time being I am still trying to get out of this jungle.

C.H. How did that set you up for when you came to Britain? You said that you found it easy in a way to start at the BBC – did they in any way resent either your blackness or your politics?

A.M. The BBC is an institution which is part of the Establishment. And we all know how much the Establishment will fight and go on fighting to preserve national traditions. I have nothing against the preservation of national traditions. But what the BBC does is not only preserve the bad as well as the good British traditions – they also perpetrate, up to this day, the antiquated colonial beliefs. In plain and simple language, the BBC resent my blackness and politics and makes no effort to conceal their resentment. If you deny what I am saying go to the BBC African Service and find out yourself. Compare the standards and quality of programmes put out to

Africa and those to Britain itself and Europe. Ask to listen to Radio Plays produced for Africans to listen to. Discuss with the producers – who are 99·999 per cent whites who have one time or another worked in colonial Africa – their harangues and morbid ideas of the African and what his needs are. Their condescensions and hypocritical flatteries.

It does not bother me now though whether the BBC resents my blackness and my politics, because I know better. I know whose interest is important to the BBC. They know where I am at and that bothers a few of them whose bread is buttered only because there are these mediocre programmes still being sent out to Africa. Nevertheless me and they play for time like cat and mouse.

C.H.   What about your experiences in Britain – first of all in terms of yourself as an individual, and then about your experiences as an individual in the world of drama?

A.M.   As an individual in my own right I know what I am doing. It might not be the best thing or the right thing, but it is the best for me and I strive in whatever I do to achieve perfection. Therefore, anybody with whom I work I genuinely demand and expect the best of them or to get the best out of them because only in that way can one perhaps in time influence some changes in this society. I don't have time to waste. But unfortunately I have discovered, and sadly, too, that in England the system doesn't want consciously professional hardworking black artists to get together and work together. Whenever black people get together outside the *guardiance* of a white leader, it is said that they are up to something political. Our coming together is always a threat. A threat in the sense that we will just, by not even knowing it, create another kind of culture which is only meant for the liberals to talk about at their groovy parties – but which they never want to see exist.

C.H.   How would you define that culture as being different: first of all you suggest it would be a different culture – well, what's the culture that exists at present, and how would the one that you would be defining differ from it?

A.M. It would be different in the sense that when they call the blackman a black Englishman he is obviously a different Englishman – he is not a root or part of the root of the tree. His contribution to the Union Jack is not a social, political thing – it's basically economic – and therefore that culture will have to be different – different in the sense that this man is in a better position to say, 'here I was born in England' or 'here I have been working in England' or 'here I have made certain contributions' and when he is able to stand outside himself and see that kind of Britain in which he is living and say, 'well, I'm going to write a play about the environment, not about black or white but about that environment', he obviously will be creating a different kind of literature, which perhaps Pinter or Osborne has not been conscious of. By the look of things in Britain, it does appear to me that white people still don't believe nor can they accept that the blackman living among them has a culture. That is a fact. Anyway, the new culture will not be talking of and identifying with characters out of James Baldwin's books or Edward Braithwaite's 'To Sir with Love'. It will not be like Jews in Germany going underground to fight Nazism or fleeing. The culture I am talking about will be all-embracing. Embracing in the sense that the British public will not be allowed to persecute blacks in England while the rest of the Third World make appeals to the UN on behalf of human rights and civil liberties.

No. Now we know where the strength lies. Britain might rank among world power, possess industrial power, etc., etc., but where does the raw material come from? Culture is not just 'Social – Social'. It is many things and means many things.

C.H. Trying to pin you down, could you say at what point your colour within this society impinges on your activities as an artist? First of all, do you regard this society as a racist society?

A.M. It's obvious I don't have to regard it as one because I did not create this society and what is happening to me and why I react to the society the way I react is something that has already been motivated by forces which are greater than me because I am talking as an individual. So I believe that this society does not really directly influence me because I am ostracized as an artist and as a man. The critics yet have to develop a kind of vocabulary whereby they can come and see me with other black artists performing together on their own rights and merits, and not as a black company doing the wild savage thing. We must be allowed to make mistakes, because no community, even the Arts Council, none of the so-called local and national and commercial financiers make money readily available for us blacks to do a decent production.

C.H.   One of the implications of what you've been saying though is that you want to be allowed, and even financed, to do your own thing collectively as blacks. Earlier on you were saying you didn't want to be defined as black, but the implications of what you're saying is that because you're regarded as black you're not allowed to do what you want.

A.M.   You must understand that 'when a play is produced at the National Theatre or the RSC' there is supposedly a very high standard and that is white standard, and it is also a white artistic standard, and therefore the educated audience who come to the theatre are in the majority white people who, too, have white standards and expect the white traditional standard. To go below that standard would be unforgivable. I don't think the RSC or the National would dare attempt to do so. What I am saying is that under the given circumstances, genuine challenging work for the black artist in the RSC or the National is only the dream of a lunatic. This reflects on the standard of the black actor, in fact, the black actor is meant to have no standard at all. They are not supposed to create a standard of their own – they are not supposed to create a challenge – they are not allowed to make mistakes – they are not even given the chance to try to make mistakes, and so therefore there is no black art or black literature or black standard that is readily accepted or given the chance to risk making mistakes in the white man's world. Peter Brook can loose a thousand or two thousand – Sir Laurence can –

but can I? Nobody would lift a finger to give me £500 to do a production because from the very onset they don't think that I know anything about theatre, and even the drama schools, when you go there, they don't think that you have the talent and ability to really measure up to expectations. The whole thing is a white national reaction – a conspiracy to keep the blacks out. Australians come here and make great successes and are given the chance to work as decent, respectable, hardworking artists. But if I were to say to Anni Domingo, a black actress, 'Come and play for me', say in *Macbeth*, not *Black Macbeth*, or for that matter *Hamlet*, and I asked her to play Ophelia, they wouldn't think she's got the mentality, the personality, training and the artistic talent to do the part.

C.H. Just because she's black?

A.M. Yes. They think you've got a black brain, a black mind – everything about us is black. But not only the blackness, no it goes far, far deeper. We are just not human in every sense of the word. We are a humbug.

C.H. In this country because you are defined as black and alien what you want to say in a way is a rejection of that definition – a rejection of the stigma that a racist society tries to impose on you – so in a way you have a need to state the integrity of blackness, don't you?

A.M. There was Obi Egbuna who tried in his own way to explain black integrity. What did they do with him? The whites? They hounded him. Locked him up. Trumped up charges against him.

Sorry, I don't have time to preach black integrity to white insolence. I am not Martin Luther King. I don't go where white liberals think I should. I don't talk with the tongue of the Holy Spirit. What happened to Egbuna in England is a lesson or should be a lesson to all blacks who are committed to have justice. To right the wrongs done to the poor, exploited and suffering, I will not be bribed, cheated or fooled to waste my time, effort and energy taking coal to Newcastle! Let it be said here and now that I'm not saying either that I want the

British people to say 'you are not black – you are Amadu Maddy' – I think it is very welcome for them to call me black.

C.H. I suppose the problem is that the black British do exist as a category – they exist as a category who are discriminated against as blacks ever have been – and your wish to tell people that your are an African or that someone else is a Jamaican is to insist that blacks are not simply just tinted Englishmen – which is what England demands of them, isn't it?

A.M. I wish the English people would demand more of themselves in an honest way as they do those blacks who come here to help them out of their mess.

C.H. Well, earlier on we talked about difficulties of being black in this country in the sense that in a racist society you're always faced with the problem of being given a definition of yourself – you are black. Now tell me about the people who as you said have natural talents, and as far as the British are concerned are blacks, and the difficulties they have in getting parts which are acceptable to them, or the sorts of parts they're offered – tell me from your own experience what sort of parts you get?

A.M. Well, I am out of this because I don't act on television or on radio or in the theatre in plays produced by the big managements or in the fringe theatres or in the BBC or ITV because when you see a black man on television, and this goes back as far as 1960 when I came to England, by the time you say 'look at him' – he's gone – the sort of pointing finger parts. And if he's on the stage he's there to say 'Madam' or 'Missus' or 'Bwana' – it is a pity but again one understands because as I said earlier the average Englishman or the average artistic Britisher who controls or works for the media does not take black artists seriously – and they claim, when questioned, that black artists are lazy and not serious with their work.

Anyway being what I am, knowing that I take myself and my work very seriously, I have sort of set up my own little theatre company and I do my own plays, and when I do my own plays I act in them and I direct them – I even do my own costumes – I do them the way I want. I remember they wanted to do one of my plays and this fellow at the BBC – I think BBC2 – was going to tell me what I should write and how the play should be written. I do not make that kind of compromise, not for money or prestige. I don't think I can, but at the same time he was a very young fellow – a liberal – a sort of 'Yes, man, we're all brothers' you know – I don't consider a white man my brother – I don't – just like that I do not readily accept when a black man meets me in the street and says 'Hi brother man – groove' – I don't 'groove' with soap-box prophets and verbal demonstrators who merely demonstrate their fraternity to convince the watching but uninterested public. Nevertheless, black actors are in this position where, because of want of money, and if you like love of their so-called profession, they have to take parts in demoralizing plays which depict them as sub-humans in every conceivable respect as the white writer thinks of the black man – somebody who's singing – somebody who's got white teeth to show, and somebody who can jump around doing hula-hula – this is what has and still is going on. Unfortunately there are the old type of black actors who would readily go and do a television or film production for money, and once it's finished you know, it's finished. Just recently, and this is my own latest experience because I've never put myself in such a position – they were going to do 'The Explorer' in Gabon; actually they didn't want me in the production as an actor or anything of that kind, but as someone who knows something about African history. I turned up and after talking to the producer he offered me a sort of leading part and also asked me if I would like to co-direct the production. Two days later on a Sunday I was called up in the afternoon to meet Lord Snowdon – I met Lord Snowdon in Kensington and we had a drink and we had something to eat and we talked about 'Mary Kingsley' about my work, I accepted – I was in fact flattered to co-direct a television documentary with Lord Snowdon. I insisted on getting the script – the working script – I never got it – I got a letter saying 'yes' it's been confirmed that I would co-direct and they were going to pay me £200.

Now I thought this was a big insult. I called the chap who'd signed the letter: 'Don't ever write a letter to me directly, you write to the agent who recommended me. I do not leave London without £150 a day as a co-director, because I know what it is to direct, and I know how much I am worth, and I am not learning to direct in England, I've been doing it on the continent.' The BBC refused to pay this amount. I told them I was not going to co-direct. Then, later I was bullied to sign the acting contract to go to Gabon, they were offering me £351 to go to Gabon for four weeks, I stated: 'This money is not enough' and they went on and on and I said 'O.K., since I've turned down co-directing I will go.' They offered to pay £5 allowance money in Gabon – a day – that's outside the £351. All day I had insisted on getting the script because I wanted to know what part I would be playing. When I got the script it had nothing to do with Mary Kingsley. I called one of the assistants to the producer and I said, 'Look, whoever wrote that script tell them that I do not agree with it and I think it's stupid for the BBC to call on somebody like me to do such a part – they should know that I do not just work for money. But another black actor took the job, therefore one cannot talk on behalf of black actors. However, it is a pity that anything they do that is seen on radio or TV is so bad – bad because it has got nothing to do with the situation in which they are living in England – it has got nothing to do with them as people – it has to do with them as specks of paint splashed on canvas that is actually insignificant – nobody would see that speck – it's only the painter who sees it. To the white writer who writes these things it means a lot – but I have yet to meet an English writer who has really met a black person in the flesh and really got to know them and write something about them. It is impossible for me to put myself up and talk on behalf of blacks. I know that they are not paid enough, that Equity has got no interest in them,* that BBC radio, television, ITV whatever you like, only use them when they want them – they are not interested in them at all – not one

*After this conversation was taped, Equity produced a report on the difficulties experienced by their black members.

bit, because they believe that their white jobs will go on – their white art will go on without these black people – these people are not even black seagulls in their white nightmare, in their human daydreams.

C.H.   But in that sense, in the way that black actors are treated by major TV networks and broadcasting companies – is that any different from the way in which white actors are treated – do they come in for special treatment?

A.M.   I wouldn't care less how they are treated because it's their country and whether they're treated good or bad they in turn treat black actors bad. Every one of them, whether they're out of work or working, they are as bad as the liberals who invite you to tea and try to tell you how much they've done for you in terms of liberalization. They are as bad, and I mean it and I, Amadu Maddy say it, I mean it, until the day I can stand face to face with a white actor and tell him what I think in terms of art, in terms of man to man living together side by side, until then he doesn't need me and I don't need him – the white actor would be happy to see my back.

C.H.   But that's on the part of the white actor – what you're saying is the white actor basically has no sense of commitment to the particular situation that you face. What I'm wondering is, are the pressures that you face different – or in any way more difficult, more oppressive than the difficulties facing the white actor?

A.M.   There is always a chance for the white actor – there is always a chance if he is an actor – if he wants to act – if he knows what he's doing – but there is not a ghost of a chance for the black actor who really wants to work. The white actor's got any amount of chances – you see he can go to Germany to act, he can go to Denmark, he can go to Sweden, he can go to America. People like Peter Brook can enjoy it here in England, in America and in my own country, because they're experts, they're certainly experts. Well, I tell you, nobody can be an expert on me, and this is why it's a waste of time having a dialogue with white people because they don't listen to you – they don't hear you – they know what they want to say, they know what they see, they know what they understand, they pick up one little black actor and they build him up, and when they want to do away with him they do away with him and then they pick up another one – it's always one at a time – always. They never get to the heart of the matter, the root of the problem. They gloss the surface and make it so beautiful – ho, yes, you can make a joke at my blackness and I can make a joke at your being cockney, or being terribly, terribly bourgeois, or being the liberal who fornicates. And I tell you the blackman, whether you are an artist or not, you are not better than the man who sweeps the road because as a man you are looked upon as a phallic phenomenon who goes around raping, if not with your prick, you rape with your eyes.

C.H.   Presumably that's the state of the game in terms of employment – what about your opinion as a playwright about the sort of plays that blacks are invited to take part in?

A.M.   They are not actually invited to take part in plays – the day they start inviting black actors to take part in plays England would have started the beginning of the revolution – a cultural revolution. They are not invited – producers, directors, the managements, whether they're BBC or ITV, know exactly what they expect of Black John and what they expect of Black Bill – they don't look upon us as artists – we don't have representatives – we don't have a voice and so therefore we are not invited – we don't have respectable black agents that are respected and treated on the same equal standard as white agents. In fact we are a voiceless crowd in your white wilderness – we don't have a voice and so therefore we are not invited – we are summoned to appear and when you appear you know you will be given £18 – they exploit you worse than the landlords exploit you. If you want to know how Rachmanism works in England, try to become a conscientious black actor then you will know.

C.H.   What about the future just to finish off with? What would you either expect or hope for in the theatre and drama in the future in Britain in respect to race relations?

A.M. There is only one hope and that is there are quite a few small black companies springing up with black fellows as directors running their own companies. There are quite a lot of those fellows going on with no money backing them, but if a particular black actor likes my work they work with me, but they are not tied to work with me because I cannot afford to pay them, but at the same time they are at least trying to do something which they believe in. Whether it's inadequate – whether it's mediocre, it's a start. Most white directors and white agents and white producers don't come to see these productions and so they don't know what is going on, but anyway it is a start for these people and all I can say is I wish them luck. Personally, I do not look upon Britain as the place where my work will be respected or accepted – never have I at any time had a dream that I would become a 'star' or a 'great writer' – I am very content with my striving for perfection as an artist, and in doing so I hope that I make a decent human and artistic contribution. I should think that in our own ways working at what we are working at, we will try to be decent to the people we work with who are black, and at the same time strive for the best, the best in what we have and create our standard. Because until we can create a standard of our own it is impossible for whites in England to take us seriously, for as I said time and time again, nobody thinks of us as people that you can take seriously. We are regarded just as objects not even worthy of a place in your society, let alone our natural human existence.

C

PART III

In this section Jennie Laishley, a social psychologist who has worked in the field of race relations and education, uncovers the bias found in the books, comics and textbooks to which children are daily exposed. John Downing, a sociologist with long involvement in race relations, provides detailed evidence of the bias in the television news and current affairs programmes and examines the significance of this for a class-based society. Finally, Graham Faulkner, a psychologist with research experience in the area of race relations, focuses upon the particular critical impact of the British mass media upon Asian adolescents. Though the focus of their contributions is varied it is apparent how each contributor is isolating different aspects of the same phenomenon, namely the emergence of racist bias in the mass media. There is also a common concern for the consequences such bias can have.

4. The Images of Blacks and Whites in the Children's Media

Jennie Laishley

In the 1960s in Britain it was often said that children were never prejudiced and some added that youngsters did not even notice colour or any other racial differences. This assertion relieved people of the responsibility of considering the sources of children's attitudes which might be of particular importance for the development of prejudice. However, children are not so blind to the adult world. Many young children in Britain are aware of both their own colour and that of their playmates. Initially, differences in skin colour appear to be of no more significance to them than any other physical characteristic – it is not seen as a way of distinguishing good people from bad or nice from nasty. The disturbing fact is that this early awareness without prejudice is shattered swiftly by contact with the world of older children and adults, who have developed fixed race attitudes and prejudiced ones at that. Young children imitate and they imitate the less attractive aspects of human behaviour as well as the more pleasant.

Mary Ellen Goodman, who worked in the United States in the 1950s, found three and four year olds using words like 'nigger' as insults and as swear words before they had any clear idea of Negroes as a group. A few years later when these children could understand how society was composed of groups of people and what was meant by being a member of one group rather than another, they knew the vocabulary of prejudice already. David Milner, working in two British cities in the 1960s, found the same type of behaviour in children. White children were pleased to be white and many of them did not like black children. Black children, especially the West Indian children, wanted to be white. Children were repeating adult views, like the five year old who said a black doll was 'bad' because 'he should have learnt the language before he came over here'. There is a lot of other evidence on the development of prejudiced attitudes in white British children and self-dislike and self-doubt in black boys and girls. The general picture gives cause for serious concern.

So, it is a fact that British children learn prejudice. The white children become convinced that white is good and black is bad and the black children tend to agree, with obvious consequences on how they feel about themselves. Attitudes, beliefs, opinions do not appear out of the blue. They are learnt from somebody, whether through spoken word, behaviour or written word. Individual personality may make some people more susceptible than others, but all of us are influenced to some extent. I want here to consider some of the influences on children of the written word – their media, which includes comics, fiction and schoolbooks. This covers the printed word for children from the purely entertaining to the officially educative. There are two reasons for surveying the children's media. One is that white children build up their images of the world, of groups of people and of the relations between these groups from sources such as these. Direct instruction and suggestion from adults and other children obviously play their part. However, in books, comics and magazines children are presented with ideas and people within a situation, which, in the case of schoolbooks especially, is presented as an accurate picture of life somewhere at sometime. The white children's images of other groups, and here I am particularly concerned with black groups, affects their attitudes and their behaviour. Consequently this affects the atmosphere in which black adults and children have to live, the attitudes and expectations they will meet. The second reason for looking at children's media is the direct effect it has on black children. They are told through these sources that they are of less importance than white people. If you hear yourself run down or ignored often enough it becomes very hard to still believe there is no truth in the accusations. Too many black children and adults have a low opinion of themselves or are unsure of their own abilities because they have been told so often, directly or indirectly, that they are inferior, that their culture is not important and that they will never be as capable as the majority of white people. The children's media does nothing to counteract this picture, in fact, it is one of the sources of prejudiced attitudes, both reflecting past and present attitudes and therefore contributing to future prejudice.

It is obvious that comics are published to entertain and that only the more specialized magazines aim to educate. However, just because comics are read for fun does not mean that their content goes in one ear and out the other. The intention of entertaining does not excuse comics from a scrutiny of their contents. British children buy something like ten-and-a-half million comics a week and many of them probably take the content more seriously than their schoolbooks. Learning is not something restricted to the classroom, it is an activity we carry on all the time and children undoubtedly learn ways of thinking about black people and their countries from comics. It is one of the many influences on them. For the black children, comics are one of the measures of how this country sees them and, for many born in this country, it is one of the indirect ways they have of finding out about the country from which their parents came and with which they will be at least partly associated, if not by themselves then by others.

I spent some time looking at comics for children in Britain, reading a large number of issues from 1971 and 1972. These covered comics for young children, boys' comics, girls' comics and teenage magazines. I was looking for answers to three questions relevant to both black and white readers. These were: firstly do black characters appear in the stories and serials published; secondly, if black characters appear what sort of people are they, and thirdly, what impression is given of the countries other than Britain, especially black countries? The answers I found to these questions were very discouraging.

In the 162 issues I read, only twenty stories included any black characters. Most comics carried seven or eight stories per issue, often set in foreign lands and urban areas of England, and yet only these few stories extended their characters beyond white British children or adults. Furthermore, of these twenty stories, only twelve could be said to have black characters who stood out as individuals. In the other instances, black people appeared in crowd scenes or as hostile masses. There were no black heroes and heroines, unless you count Mowgli in *Disneyland* who is a very European Indian and, anyway, changes colour from issue to issue. The most responsible and intelligent parts in which blacks appeared were as sidekicks to the white hero or heroine. Some stories had black characters who, although not villains, had very little life to them, and a limited role in the story. A common situation was black characters who were shown in an unfavourable light, either as evil criminals, treacherous natives or stupid halfwits. Furthermore, the picture given of countries like Africa or India was limited and misleading, showing them as 'primitive' in a way which showed no understanding of cultural differences and which only encourage attitudes in children which would be highly ethnocentric – that is to say, grounded in their own culture and regarding their own as the best of all.

Some examples from comics will illustrate the way in which they contribute to the images of black people and their countries. An example of the type of treatment Africa and Africans receive appeared in the boys' comic *Smash*. This serial, 'The Fighting Three', told of three white main characters who were described as being 'in darkest Africa'. Africans appeared as the Obijoes, stupid and ineffective savages, who were referred to as 'natives' and once as 'you big ape'. They were tamed by one of the white men, whom they worshipped for his resemblance to their idol. This is so often the only image that children hold of Africa and its inhabitants, not realizing that it is a country of contrasts, with development alongside traditional life and that the latter is not an idiot's paradise. Such a story cannot be treated as just fun when there is no contrast to this picture. Africa treated in serials

set in the present appeared no different than Africa of the past
– hostile and uncivilized except where white influence prevails.
A one-issue story in *Princess Tina*, called 'Warrior's Child',
told of a Boer Trek in the 1830s. The black characters were
'fierce Hottentot warriors' of whom it was said 'even among
themselves these terrible people make war'. The happy ending
to the story was engineered by the kind act of a white girl and
the story, not very surprisingly, made no comment on white
hostility in Africa, on the fact that whites were taking over
land that did not belong to them or that the course of subsequent race relations in this part of the world is nothing to
be proud of.

Child readers are given a woefully inaccurate and biased
view. For white children this confirms their beliefs from other
sources that black Africans are savages in hostile tribes who
attack without reason but can be won over by superstition
or simple gifts. For the black child who is African or West
Indian in origin, these stories have serious implications for
how they see themselves – are they inferior to whites? How
can they relate to a past and present which is peopled by black
morons and insurgents?

Another serial, this time from *June and School Friend*,
showed another side to the image presented in comics of
black people, especially Africans. The serial, 'Safari Hotel',
was set 'deep in the African bush' and showed an Africa
dominated by whites. White people managed the hotel, the
servants were black. White faces dominated the town scenes,
whilst black faces predominated in the 'jungle village of
Darhuzin', with drums, grass huts and rotund village chief.
The area doctor was white, his subordinate (not assistant)
was black. The highest status black character was the local
safari policeman, but it was not he, but the white heroine and
the white doctor, who subdued the rampaging black locals.
A story like this is likely to add to any feelings of white
superiority in the mind of the child reader, whatever their
colour. It is the whites who hold responsible positions in a
black country and keep a friendly eye on the child-like
Africans. There are now a large number of African countries

run by black Africans and yet of the four stories I read, set entirely in Africa, all situations described were totally white-dominated. This picture of the world hits the black child hard in a society which is as colour conscious as Britain. They are likely to identify with the white hero and to reject a black identity which implies being an unintelligent and unreliable underdog.

India has tended to escape the more extremely insulting treatment that Africa has received. Indians have tended to fall into the category of subordinate but exotic and wily rather than intelligent. India is the home of the snake-charmer, beds of nails, mysterious alleyways and curry. Yet, Indian characters have scarcely any more life of their own than Africans, and India as a country is usually of no more importance than an interesting setting for a story. Indians did not appear in threatening hordes, although a pair of Indian thugs in 'Sara's Kingdom' in *Sally* showed hostile intentions which were quelled easily by the white schoolgirls at the centre of the story. There were no Indian heroes in Indian or British based stories. Indians often appeared as friendly and helpful but they were subordinate to the white characters. Only one Indian, the old Queen in 'Sara's Kingdom', was equal in status to the white schoolgirls.

Other non-European and non-white groups appeared as supporting characters, as comic/violent characters and as hostile masses. The Caribbean Voodoo people of 'Castaways on Voodoo Island' in *Tammy* are dangerous people who have, in the event, been fooled by a white man. Even the black criminals who had some individual existence tended to be subordinate to a boss white criminal, for example in 'Fishboy' in *Buster*, where the character makes comments like 'Him plenty unconscious, boss! Much good shot with boomerang.' The black characters who appear more favourably than those mentioned so far show up further limitations of the images of blacks in comics. These people are not evilly-intentioned and they show some intelligence and resourcefulness, but they are never the hero of a story or even of any importance to the storyline. As a consequence they are not sufficient to offset the bad influence of the really unfavourable black characters. For instance, *Princess Tina* ran a nursing serial called 'Ross – student nurse'. In a few episodes a black staff nurse appeared in the background. Many readers probably did not notice her, and, although she was above the white heroine in nursing rank, her importance to the events in the story was negligible. Similarly, in a serial called 'Sindy' in *June and School Friend,* the white heroine's American Indian friend had a role in the story but was of less importance than Sindy. In a boys' comic, *Smash,* a serial about Britain in the near future showed white hero, Simon Kane, with a West Indian assistant called Tubby. Tubby certainly had a degree of resourcefulness and technical skill but Kane was the brains of the outfit. Tubby called him 'Boss' or 'Mr Kane' and Kane called him 'Tubby' – Tubby did the fetching and carrying. If there were a few black Simon Kanes and white Tubbys, such a story as this would not be reason for complaint. But this is not the case. The limited casting of black characters limits children's images to the savage or childlike black and the black who does well under white guidance. It is even rare to find black characters in teenage girls' magazines, if not a non-existent occurrence. This is a situation where pictures of black groups and singers are appearing with articles on other pages but their fictional counterparts never enter into the romances comprising the rest of the comic.

The reason for criticizing the content of comics is its lack of balance as regards black and white characters. White people appear across the range of human types. You find the criminal, the clown, the mysterious, but also the everyday type of person, the intelligent and the dashing hero or heroine. Black characters are limited to unfavourable and foolish characters and to characters who are of less significance than the white characters dominating the serials. Added to this is the picture given of the countries from which black peoples come. Some examples of black countries as primitive backwaters and as dominated by whites have already been given and the situation is neatly summed up by a series which appeared for the younger child in *Sunny Stories.* The two characters in what was essentially a travelogue were white. They journeyed around the world but saw only two instances of non-white peoples – a child from an island in the Java sea and some Mexican Indians. No black inhabitants appeared in East Africa, India, South America or South Africa, although white residents did appear. The picture given of the world was that of a white world.

Criticism of the dearth of good black characters in children's comics of the treatment of black countries applies equally to children's fiction, both for the younger and the older child. Fiction is another source of the images which white and black children build up. Here again, by books set in Britain black characters are conspicuous by their absence, with the exception of a very few writers, modern books do not take account of the multi-racial nature of the British population. Books set abroad include almost exclusively white characters, blacks appearing as servants, natives and exotic or restless locals. One would not expect older books set in Britain to include black characters, coloured migration to Britain is a relatively recent phenomenon, but the change that has occurred in the population is sufficient reason for parents and teachers to seek out good modern books which include black as well as white characters, for white readers as well as black.

A number of surveys have been done on children's literature and on readers for the younger child. Ken Worpole, for instance, looked at the Ladybird Series and found its pages full of white, middle-class parents and their children, living in detached houses with gardens. A very limited view of the world was being communicated to children. Books on other countries tended to show the same faults as I have criticized in comics. For example, one Ladybird on African History had the white characters being told how 'horrible' slavery was until 'Britain took a stand . . . The British came here to stop the slave trade and eventually we took over East Africa.' Britain seemed to come out of the situation very well, especially since she was thoroughly involved in the slave trade and the wealth of ports like Bristol was built on that trade! The idea given is of a benovolent Britain saving black Africa and then kindly dominating the country because the blacks were too dim to take care of themselves.

Fiction for younger children is generally all-white in its characters, as are the readers which are used with children learning to read. I have come across only four multiracial readers-series which make an attempt to portray children of different colours and nationalities. One wonders how many schools are using them. What is more likely is that the all-white, largely middle-class series prevail and some of the series still to be found in schools include the more blatantly prejudiced comments of older books. For instance, the Fundamental Readers Scheme, which has still been discovered in primary schools, includes this example. White Tommy is told, 'I should go to the Nigger Minstrels . . . They all look very funny. Their faces were black as coal but their hands were not black.' Tommy asks then, 'Do black men ever wash?' The chance of young children encountering material like this is disturbing given the beliefs about black people, namely that they are dirty and that their main accomplishment is entertaining white people. The readers of these books for the young child are black and white and children develop their first notions of what the world is like, of the place in life and relative importance of people, of who gives and who takes the orders from sources like readers and fiction. As with comics, children are shown in their readers a predominantly white world and a white-dominated world.

Janet Hill, a London librarian, undertook with other librarians a comprehensive survey of fiction for seven to eleven year olds. They concentrated on fiction set in the countries from which the main migrants to Britain came. The picture that emerged was depressing. With the exception of a few really good books, much of children's fiction about other countries, especially black countries, was prejudiced in its content, misleading or just plain boring. The attitudes conveyed by the books were such as to encourage children in patronizing ways of looking at black people and black countries and some of the comments appearing in the books were downright insulting. A story set on a South African orange farm (*Dry River Farm* by W. M. Levick) gives an example of this sort of treatment in the comment:

'The taps of the water tanks near the house had been locked in case anyone should be wasteful of the precious drinking water, for natives are extraordinarily careless, even when food and drink are very scarce.' The white son of the farmer in the same story did not understand the social status of black and white and asked if a black boy could come to his school. His father patiently answered:

'Listen, old chap, let me see if I can explain. It's all so difficult, Filiki isn't ready yet for school!'

The paternalism of the white man in Africa and elsewhere is therefore communicated to children and insult is cloaked in apparent kindness and concern. Black Africans may be faithful retainers or the 'benighted heathen' which trouble Biggles but so few books have black men as masters in their own land. Books with some historical basis vary in the images they convey. Janet Hill describes several books which purport to recount events in the past of, say, Africa, but which concentrate exclusively on the exploits of white men. An exception to this was a book on *African Heroes* by N. Mitchison, a story of black heroes dogged by white exploitation of Africa, by deception and cruelty. Books of this calibre can contribute to a genuine understanding in children of the background to the present situation, to appreciation of ways of life very different to the Western model and, in Africa in particular, to the situation under apartheid. If children come to read such books as these, they offer a counter balance to the images developed through reading the biased books. However, there is a heavy load to counteract and the subtler forms of prejudice are just as dangerous as the more blatant. A tale of two teenage girls on holiday in South Africa (In *Nothing Happened At All* by J. Shaw), included a brief discussion of apartheid, where they agreed that Africans were being treated unfairly. Yet two days later, they visited a 'native township' to see 'the other side of the medal'. They helped their aunt to dole out bread, peanut butter and milk to children and one of the girls commented:

'And often after that, when I caught sight of Aunt Helen, that immaculately groomed woman, at a party, say, or doing the flowers, or entertaining people in her pretty sitting room, I thought of her that morning with the little black children up to her elbows in peanut butter.' So the child reader is given a dash of patronizing sympathy, a brief Lady Bountiful visit to the natives and then back to the comfortable *status quo*. Children are given the impression that black people should be the object of pity rather than active help because their situation under apartheid is not really that bad. For the black child this is further evidence that it is only white people who ever have the power, along with the pretty sitting rooms.

Black Africans appear to be the most badly represented in children's fiction, if only perhaps because Africa appears to be a favourite setting for stories, especially adventure stories. However, the Arabs in Africa are provided with an uncomplimentary image in books in which they appear. They appear as fawning and treacherous in *Algerian Adventure* by D. King. This book starts from the premise that no Arab can be trusted and the schoolboys are warned by the teachers about the 'dusky men and boys' selling trinkets on the ship:

'I don't want you boys to speak to any of the Arabs, though. I know it's fun to get them to talk, and to listen to their broken English, but some of them are strange fellows and their ways are not our ways, so don't try to make friends with them.'

Again the images that children are likely to build up from such material are ethnocentric, namely they are likely to regard their own culture as the yardstick for measuring any other cultures, the British way being the best, and it being quite reasonable to expect everyone to speak good English. Wogs begin at Calais, or perhaps the Gibraltar Straits.

The tales of Pakistan and India reviewed by Janet Hill and her fellow-librarians contributed sometimes to unfavourable pictures of Indians, largely as fawning and subservient to the white men in India. However, often the story, although set in

India, gave so little information of the country that it could just as well have been set elsewhere. India was not shown as a country inhabited by Indians. The halcyon days of sahibs, natives and tiger hunts are giving way in some of the newer books to more realistic stories, although modern town life and its problems is sometimes overshadowed by the more picturesque side of village life. However, the days of the sahib and the North-West frontier still appear. In A. M. Westwood's story, *Jungle Picnic*, three nieces of 'a wealthy English sahib' visit India. At one point in the plot an Indian guide kills a rampaging tiger and is rewarded by being sent to school by the uncle. When told this, the guide is overcome with gratitude – 'the palms of his thin brown hands came together, and he bent and touched Uncle Jasper's feet'. The images therefore developed by white and black children are along the lines discussed already and it becomes clearer how many aspects of the children's media combine together to encourage feelings of white superiority in white children and black inferiority influencing the way black children see themselves. There is little of value for an Indian child to identify with if his main source of information on India is the books available to him from English bookshelves.

The West Indies has not attracted the writers of adventure stories as Africa has and the range of books available on the Caribbean, especially for the younger child, are few. Again, of the selection available, some perpetuate an inaccurate image of the area. The less well conceived books present these islands as a tropical island paradise, with sun, sea and discreetly hidden locals, whose poverty contrasting with the splendour of tourism is often left unsaid. Since many adults and children have this image of the Caribbean, they often fail to understand why West Indians leave their islands to live in Britain. Not knowing anything of the employment situation in the Caribbean or of British influence there, they ask why West Indians left the sunshine and beaches to come to a foreign land.

All the books in Janet Hill's survey were set in countries other than Britain – the extent of books set in Britain with black characters is very small. Many of the books available set abroad contribute to children's attitudes in an unfavourable fashion, perpetuating images of black people which are derogatory and patronizing and giving a picture of black countries as largely white areas. Their influence can be added on to that of children's comics. Undoubtedly, some good books do exist, but how many children get to read them and how far do they counteract the influence of the badly conceived fiction?

A group of teachers, calling themselves Teachers Against Racism, have become involved in criticizing publicly the books for young and older children which portray black characters in an insulting fashion. Their much publicized prime target has been *Little Black Sambo* which probably sums up many people's notions, conscious or unconscious, of black people of African and West Indian origin. Other characters which have been criticized have been the evil Golliwogs of the Enid Blyton Noddy series. They are the only black characters in the series and a source of danger rather than just mischievousness. When one has heard young children and older referring to black children and adults as 'golliwog' or 'fuzzifuzzi', it becomes clear that the Golliwogs of Noddy fame are not a ludicrous example.

From fiction I want to move on to school textbooks. When one finds again the same unfavourable images of black people and the same picture of white-dominated black countries, it is obvious that this prejudice is firmly entrenched in the British culture and traditions, permeating the literature, entertainment and education media. Historical events, especially past colonial relationships, have left a legacy of belief in white superiority, of patronage and charitable pity and of out and out hostile prejudice, which are supported by beliefs about the personal characteristics and abilities of what were black colonial peoples. It has been said that the history and culture of England could be reconstructed from its children's books. Old relationships, incorporated into present attitudes, live on in the pages of books and comics. Biggles is alive and well and still fighting the heathen, genteel memsahibs and intrepid white explorers still control the ever restless natives. In this situation, children's school books place a covering of 'fact' over the fiction. Textbooks show the same biases and prejudices of comics and books but they are presented as accounts of real life past and present.

School textbooks can be criticized on three grounds in their contribution to beliefs and images about black people and their countries. These are that they present out-dated facts, biased presentation of events and inaccurate or blatantly prejudiced images of black groups. Obviously the older books have facts and statistics which are out of date but even new and supposedly revised books sometimes give independent countries their old colonial names and ignore or skim over post-independence history. The existence of older books in the schools is a reflection of the lack of finance or willingness to spend on up-to-date books, as well as a lack of awareness of the influence of the content of books on children's attitudes. The Education Publisher's Council in a 1971 survey found that the majority of local education authorities spent below what the Council considered to be a reasonable level of spending on books, some of the authorities spent substantially less than half the recommended level. This means that the likelihood of newer books reaching schools is lessened – publishers will not produce new series if the demand is not there. It is worth noting that publishers will sometimes take note of criticisms of textbooks and make minor alterations in new editions. However, financial considerations prevent large scale change.

The misrepresentation and biased selection of events in textbooks is disturbing in its extent and tends to become most obvious in the history books. It is unusual for a child to be given any information on pre-colonial Africa, India, the Caribbean or America, and this is the fault of the curricula as much as the books. Everything that is deemed to be of significance starts when the Europeans arrive. The interpretations for their arrival differ. R. J. Unstead (*People in History*) gave an altruistic reason. He describes Livingstone's vision of the Zambezi as 'a high road into the heart of Africa, up which Christian missionaries, trade and civilisation might travel'. The new Penguin Education series on Modern Britain is rather more honest – 'at the end of the nineteenth century the European countries became interested in building empires for themselves in tropical Africa and they decided to share out the continent.' But even this statement is baldly stated and given the information available to children, one suspects that they may not regard this as a particularly reprehensible action. Selection of events once the whites have arrived is skewed totally to the British or European standpoint. White explorers 'discover' Africa, missionaries 'civilize' black peoples, white educators, administrators and the military obliterate existing cultures under the premise that the British way is the best. The military victories are those won by the British, the atrocities and perfidies, like the Black Hole of Calcutta, are perpetrated by the other side. There are no black heroes in the British textbooks about Africa or India. Robert Clive and Livingstone are the important figures. The events of slavery are presented in terms of what Britain achieved in fighting the trade, not in terms of her part in this commerce. All in all the images provided by children's literature and by their comics are given 'factual' support by the material in textbooks. The events of history as they are shown in these books support views of black peoples as incompetent, untrustworthy and as naturally in need of white rule and guidance. Geography books tend to further this image by dealing with black countries in terms of 'primitive' techniques and 'quaint' traditional ways of life and the white countries in terms of the technological advance and industrialization, ignoring some of the quaint ways of life in the West. Even where urbanization, change and contrast in black countries are discussed, illustrations to the text tend to nullify any possible modifications in attitudes. Pygmies and Kalahari Bushmen tend to predominate, possibly because non-white ethnic groups are seen as a source of interesting information on ways of life very different to the Western. This is all very well if the full range of modes of living in black countries is given and if they are not presented as implicitly inferior to the white, Western way and this comparison to the detriment of the non-white country is all too often the tenor of description.

The pro-white selection and bias in school textbooks is supported by comments in the text. Images are built up of black people as essentially simple, subservient, childlike creatures, grateful for the crumbs from the white man's table and happy under his rule. The following are examples from books written in the 1930s, which still appear in the classrooms and were supposedly revised by the publishers in the 1950s and 1960s. That such statements pass revision is a serious comment on the revision process.

L. Edna Walter in *Work In Other Lands* described the Pygmies in Central Africa like this:

'They have black skins. Their hair is curly and grows close to their heads. Their lips are thick and red. When they dance they tap themselves and sing in queer sounds. They will dance or do anything for the white hunter because they know he will give them tobacco and salt and perhaps arrows as well.'

The assumptions are totally ethnocentric. The Pygmies are judged totally from the white Western standpoint and therefore are seen as strange because they are different and they supposedly venerate the white intruder like a dog his master. It is quite likely that the Pygmies regarded the white hunter as a quaint, white skinned, floppy-haired idiot with thin, pale lips, who was foolish enough to part with unusual and valuable goods in exchange for a very everyday dance routine. But this is not the impression which children develop. That the black people are as amused by the white as the white is by them or that they are simply being hospitable is ignored in favour of interpretations which make the white appear superior. Exploitation by whites of black people is often explained away. In the same book, it is said:

'The darkies who grow cotton are happy people with few cares. The planter looks very carefully after his darkies . . . Long, long years ago many of the darkies were slaves. Even then, very many of them were happy, for they are an easy-going people.'

The same view was given of the Ceylon tea plantations – black locals happy under a white boss. This attitude is a common one in history and geography books on black countries. It is still argued that it was all right for black people to work on the West Indies sugar plantations rather than whites, because the former were more used to the sun and did not mind this work. Similarly, one comes across bland statements about white men being necessary for the skilled and technical work in advanced industry of black countries, whilst thousands of African labourers can do the heavy un-skilled work. Supporting this view is the assumption that although the black countries have advanced somewhat in the last few years, 'they will still need our help for some time to come'. The fact that white 'help' is far from being totally philanthropic is ignored. Hence, again the image is per-petuated for the black and white readers of these textbooks that the skill and cultural advance derives from the whites and the blacks follow a long way behind.

For the black child, the history and geography lesson, not to mention other subjects, can become a lesson in inferiority and this information is not from fiction but supposed reliable school books. Think about how an African child would feel reading something like this, from W. G. Moss' *People And Homes In Other Lands*:

'Besides being the home of many wild animals, the African grasslands are the homes of many different tribes of Negroes.'

This fits all too easily into the belief of black peoples as inferior and even close to animals. Their countries are dangerous and untamed places. For instance, a geography book published in 1969 for the seven to ten year old had this to say about New Guinea:

'Does New Guinea sound like an unpleasant place? Before Europeans arrived with their sprays to kill insects, injections to prevent disease and medicines to cure the sick, it certainly was.'

What children do not read of is the less pleasant side to European activities – the exploitation alongside the aid, the spreading of disease in some areas like South America and the imposition of an alien way of life on the indigenous population. Because of these omissions, black and white children develop an overly flattering notion of white progress and of civilization. A pig-headed ethnocentricism is likely to be the result in the white children and a rejection of black roots and shame of black culture in the black children. Attempts to counteract this effect on black children have been made by some of the Black Power groups concerned about the loss of black culture for children through this sort of brainwashing. The effect on the white children is just as worrying because it is their attitudes which go to make the atmosphere in which black children and adults have to live. It is an uphill struggle, against such helpful remarks as:

'The natives are as destructive as baboons but it is very difficult to get them to change their habits' (F. Morris and R. W. Brooker in *The Earth – Man's Heritage*).

The same could be said of white men, both in terms of destructiveness and the tenacity with which they hold to their habits and their attitudes.

The self-righteous and blinkered outlook of the textbooks available for British children cannot be excused by saying that British children are only interested in British history. There are many black British children who have at least some of their roots abroad. Furthermore, the British past is thoroughly intertwined with that of the peoples who were colonized and it is high time it was realized that to talk incessantly of the British in India, the British in Africa and the British in the Caribbean, is leading children to develop a concept of those countries and their peoples as either non-existent or of no consequence until the British arrived. It is necessary to give pre-colonial and post-independence history of Third World countries, to give more than just a patronizing few words on indigenous life and culture in geography and to be more honest and less bigoted over non-Christian religions of the world. It is necessary in short to take black people and their countries seriously. The feeble argument usually wheeled out at this stage is that such a move would be brainwashing children. The ludicrousness of such a stand should by now be obvious. The children's media are at present feeding children rigid and prejudiced attitudes through the material they use and the way it is presented. Children are now being given very one-sided views of the world and their books, textbooks included, are very far from being objective. It is hardly objective to say, as in a 1960s history book, that the blowing of mutineers from the mouths of cannons in India can be partly excused as 'more humane than lengthy hanging'.

What is so disturbing is the effort needed to get people to see the effect that the attitudes and images in children's comics, books and textbooks have on children and adolescents over a protracted period of time. Dorothy Kuya at the Liverpool Community Relations Commission has organized pressure inside and outside her own area – collecting evidence, talking to teachers and parents and writing to publishers. The extent of the inertia on the subject was shown by a letter which was circulated to all Chief Education Officers by a parliamentary pressure group on Education and Race Relations in October 1971. The officers were asked if they had considered the age of the books in their schools, the information and attitudes in them and their probable contribution to race prejudice in the pupils. Apart from a minority who understood the problem and seemed to be making some attempt to change the situation, there was a vast majority of Chief Education Officers who shunted off responsibility to the teachers, or who professed themselves unable to see what it all had to do with them because they had no immigrants in their schools!

I want to end on a practical note. Following is a list of the sort of points to consider when looking at textbooks in particular, although many of the questions are applicable to comics and fiction as well. These questions cover most of the areas where the damage is done to children's attitudes and to their images of black people and countries – damage for black children and for white. Ask yourself these questions when you come across children's material:

1. In reference books and children's encyclopedias, how is 'race' defined, how are different races shown in illustrations, how far are races seen to mix one with another?

2. In what sort of way is a book written – what is the writer's attitude? Is it patronizing, condescending, insulting? What terms and language are used for different races? Are certain personalities regarded as 'typical' of certain peoples? Is the book written from one nation's point of view?

3. What type of people are most prominent in the book? Do white people predominate in black countries? Who are the heroes and who are the villains?

4. What range of information is given in the books – Do history books emphasize colonial history? Do geography books emphasize rural rather than urban development in black countries? What information is given on traditional customs and culture? What is seen as being 'progress' and 'civilization?'

5. Have books pre-1960s been updated? Are statistics, maps and facts up to date?

6. What variety is implied in the African and Asian continents? Is the wide range of peoples and cultures shown? How is South Africa or Rhodesia shown – as a white state? What attitude is shown towards apartheid?

7. How does modern-day Britain appear? Do black groups appear? How is immigration treated? Is Britain still portrayed as a very powerful nation? Is international interdependence shown?

8. In Religious materials, what is the content of hymns, prayer books and books on religion? How are black peoples treated? Are non-Christian religions mentioned and if so in what way?

9. Does the writer make any attempt to counteract old colonial attitudes? To discuss prejudice and its role in the world? Does the writer point to areas of very recent change?

The above questions are a start for people concerned about

the contribution of the children's media to insulting and patronizing images of blacks, images developed and believed by white and black child alike. Some good fiction and some improved textbooks are now available, although it is hard to see much change in comics and their characters. However, such change as has occurred to date is only a very small beginning. The images which the majority of children are still developing from their reading matter can probably be best summed up by a 'poem', written in my autograph book by a fellow pupil when we were at primary school. It went like this:

> God made the little nigger boys
> He made them in the night
> He made them in a hurry
> And forgot to paint them white.

Further Reading

Janet Hill – *Books for Children: The Homelands of Immigrants in Britain*, published by The Institute of Race Relations.

Impact: World Development in British Education, edited by Lydia White, published by Voluntary Committee on Overseas Aid and Development, 69 Victoria Street, London SW1.

Monthly Circular *Education and Community Relations*, free from The Community Relations Commission, 15–16 Bedford Street, London WC2. (Has information often on books and textbooks as well as general news.)

5. The (Balanced) White View

or

How British television opens up public discussion about racism, without Blacks*

John Downing

In Britain, where pride in democratic government is fairly usual, a key element in that pride is the existence of 'free' media. Broadcast media are thought especially significant in this connection, since they are harder to attack as reflections of conservative and capitalist interests than is the press. 'Balance' or 'fairness', and democracy, are taken to be inter-linked. An acid test of this glorification of the British social structure is the extent to which the public is to be found participating in the media, especially in TV, with its huge audiences and relatively high credibility and prestige. If the public discussion that is the hallmark of democracy is not encouraged by TV, or only in certain very restricted ways, then the achievements and development of British democracy are no longer something to be taken for granted. In one sense then this essay is designed to ask how formal, and how real, is British democracy. It moves beyond this purely polemical question, however, to analyse the impact of TV presentation of racism on the future development of British society.

During 1970, I systematically taped and analysed 1016 major weekday TV news bulletins, current affairs programmes and documentaries, amounting to 75 per cent of the possible total.[1] The topics covered were racism, and also industrial relations. Each item was analysed by means of a carefully prepared and standardized series of questions. One of these was: *Who speaks/is quoted, in what role?* It quickly became

*My thanks are due to Charlie Husband, Dick Hensman and Frank Campbell, for their contributions towards the argument in this essay.

apparent as the year proceeded that by this yardstick these forms of TV output principally act as a vehicle for dominant class spokesmen to address the working class. A slight exception to this rule is the utilization in industrial reporting of a tiny group of London-based top union officials. On the question of racism however there is no such ambiguity: dominant class whites dominate TV.

This pattern will be demonstrated first from the 1970 TV coverage of three African countries, namely South Africa, Zimbabwe (Rhodesia) and Nigeria. Then the coverage of racism inside Britain during that year will be analysed, with attention to the general contours of who spoke, the topics dealt with, and the capacity of white interviewers to handle such people as Wilson, Hogg (now Lord Hailsham) and Powell.

These two sections of the analysis are part and parcel of the same problem, and not simply an 'interesting' comparison and contrast. They are integrally linked for the following reasons. (1) These African countries have all been subjected to British colonial exploitation. (2) They have therefore also been utilized in the construction of racist beliefs. (3) They present today alternative strategies for white power in its search to manage the continued exploitation of blacks. (4) Images of what is happening in these African countries, and in Britain, together form a key part of the self-understanding of the white – and black – British working class. (5) In turn this self-understanding directly affects the future social, economic and political development of Britain; and developments in those other parts of the world with economic and political links with Britain.

The intention here therefore is not simply to detail and document the failings of TV on the subject of racism, national and international. It is to point out the implications of these failures for the development of British class society, and in particular for the future of black people within Britain.

The first three sections will each begin with a sketch of the basic links between Britain and the country concerned, and the way these links have shaped the social structures of South

Africa, Zimbabwe and Nigeria. Then the people asked to speak on each country will be reviewed. It will be seen from this exercise that media presentation reflects in certain important ways the continuing dominance of Britain over those countries, and that conversely it helped to insulate British TV audiences from the basic issues in each country. Subsequently, for the major part of this essay, the analysis will turn to Britain itself.

South Africa and its coverage

South Africa has a peculiar significance for Britain. Its economic (gold and diamonds) and strategic importance has long been a cornerstone of British foreign policy in Africa.[2] This explains the massive concentration of imperialist troops there during the Boer War of 1899–1902 – nearly half a million men were poured into the campaign, and £250 millions were spent, to crush Afrikaner economic independence before it challenged British hegemony. The ferocity of the war is legendary, with 20,000 Afrikaners dying in British concentration camps, and an untold – naturally – number of African lives lost.

Having savagely established British rule, postwar colonial policy was one of massive concession to the Afrikaners. During the war the British had cut African miners' wages by a third; previous to it, British policy to the African majority had been effectively indistinguishable from Afrikaner policy; and after the war, which Britain had claimed was fought partly for the defence of African rights, any areas of ambiguity which had offered some hope of advance to Africans were systematically yielded up to Afrikaner control. For instance, the Cape Province's limited franchise for 'nonwhites' was not guaranteed by the 1902 peace treaty at Vereeniging; instead, at Smuts' insistence, this was left to Afrikaner discretion after self-government (Article 8). What then happened to the franchise was of course correctly predicted by everyone. Yet one of the tragedies of this period was the way that leaders of the African, Cape Coloured and Indian communities kept appealing hopefully to London against local racism. . . .

British economic and strategic interest in South Africa has continued and expanded. Britain is the Republic's major trading partner (29 per cent of her exports); the Republic is the second largest overseas recipient of British direct investment (10 per cent), which in 1969 earned £86 millions, the highest return of any overseas country. From concentrating on mining, the pattern of British involvement has been expanding fast into manufacturing: engineering, textiles, chemicals, food-processing, cars, oil-prospecting, computers and nuclear power. Twenty-five of the country's leading hundred industrial firms are part British-owned; another twelve are direct subsidiaries.

In Britain these interests are especially well represented in the upper reaches of the Conservative Party: firms with South African links donated 20 per cent of the Party's 1970 election fund, amounting to £¼ million; and five members of the first Tory Cabinet had just previously held altogether thirty-two directorships in such firms. Class interest is international however: every other major capitalist power, the USA, West Germany, France, Japan and Italy, is also involved.

Strategically, international capitalism sees the Cape of Good Hope as critical both in relation to oil – the Suez Canal cannot cope with today's giant tankers – and in relation to naval deployment in any imperialist attack on insurgent forces (whether in southern Africa itself or elsewhere).*

For these strategic and economic reasons – the two being indissolubly linked – the official policy of capitalist States is to tut-tut about apartheid while remaining at rest with it, and indeed attaching high importance to firm relations with South Africa's government. One index of this importance is the impunity with which the SA Bureau of State Security (BOSS) is permitted to operate in Britain, harassing political

---

*In *Esquire* magazine (October 1974), Tad Szulc disclosed the 1970 US government's policy discussion document on South Africa, entitled – revealingly – 'Operation Tar Baby'. It confirms this analysis.

exiles, tapping their phones and burgling their premises. It must be in the nature of a tacit joint operation with the British Special Branch, winked at by the Home Office.

The iron development of racial and political oppression in South Africa – these two being also indissolubly linked – since 1902 is normally transformed by the British media into a scenario that closely resembles the image of South Africa supported by official British policy. That is to say, there are three leading elements in the overall presentation of what South Africa is.

First, it is presented as a country with close cultural and racial affinities in the shape of its white population. 'We' all play cricket and rugby and tennis and golf; the flow of skilled workers to South Africa from Britain is steady and sizeable; and there are relations and friends there who are described as a kind of extended racial family – our 'kith and kin'. If you can afford it, it looks a great place for a holiday. It is, in essence, a *white* affluent country: not four-fifths black and poor.

Second, it is a stable country, which holds regular (white) elections, and is not convulsed by military coups or communist revolutionaries. Third, 'it' does have this very strong belief in keeping racial groups apart, pursuing this policy with a remorseless logic that sometimes leads to 'rather violent' actions such as the Sharpeville massacre in 1960, and more often to petty restrictions on the colour line (separate ambulances, illegal sex). 'It' means the white minority, substituted as usual for the people as a whole. This policy seems very illiberal, but according to one growing strain of opinion inside Britain may have more realism to it than attempting to mix racial groups. This last view sees 'races' as a sort of unstable chemical compound that 'must' explode or separate. It is a convenient view, for it overlooks the origin of racial conflicts in the existence of white racism and the mechanisms of class society.

These understandings of South Africa and 'its' way of handling 'the colour problem' are very characteristic of British thinking, especially as stimulated by media output. South Africa therefore becomes part of Britain culturally, as well as economically and politically. This thinking has no grasp in most cases, nor is it encouraged to have, of the frustration and desperation of the black majority after 300 years of developing domination of their lives to the present extreme point. No vote. No right to strike. No right to form or join a trade union. A fraction of white wages. Huge child mortality in Africa's most 'affluent' country. Compulsory pass-cards to be carried always. Violent police. Frequent arrests. Giant informer-network. Compulsory dispersals to desolate rural scrublands, where there ensues mass malnutrition. *And* a solid guarantee that nothing will change for many decades, backed by weapons from Britain, France, Italy, West Germany. The most notorious oppression in the world, underwritten by the capitalist powers for gold and oil and their version of 'peace'.

What then happened in the TV coverage of South Africa in 1970? First of all, it took a larger slice – 29 per cent – of the total number of items on racism than did the UK itself. This is paralleled in the amount of time given it, sixteen and a quarter hours against just over fourteen hours allotted the UK. The issues which dominated the coverage of South Africa were two which most obviously affected the UK as well: whether sport should be played with South African teams selected on a racist basis; and whether the UK should sell arms to the minority white regime. These issues accounted for 231 (74 per cent) of the items on South Africa. To a certain extent, 1970 may be thought of as an atypical year for coverage of South Africa, since both issues were more or less peculiar to that year. On the other hand, they offered an unusual opportunity to UK television to demonstrate what it would do to explain the issues to the British public.

On the (vacuous) definitions of balance offered by spokesmen for British broadcasting, TV coverage of South Africa in 1970 achieved a minor miracle. In the sample there were 224 individuals, groups or institutions who spoke or were quoted, in a total of 533 occasions within 202 programmes (news bulletins, current affairs items, documentaries). (In another 80 news bulletins, only the newscaster spoke.) Of these 224 participants, 22 were unclassifiable as belonging to one side or the other. That left 101 participants who supported the white minority regime in general, or sports events between its racially selected emissaries and the UK, or the UK's sale of arms to the regime. Their support was stated on 252 occasions. Complementarily, precisely 101 participants in some way indicated their opposition or reserve toward the regime – on 251 occasions!

Such 'balance' is perhaps a freak, in that TV editors would be unlikely to have planned it as finely as this. However, without further analysis, these figures obliterate the outstanding feature of coverage of South Africa on TV: *only 10 per cent of the participants and 9 per cent of the statements were by black people.* Do British TV editors assume most black people have had their vocal cords cut? Or simply that they are irrelevant on a matter which so closely concerns them? Or that they cannot be trusted to speak intelligibly?

In a count of the individuals who spoke most often, the scores were as follows:

Vorster	24	Kaunda	11
Peter Hain	23	Cheetham (white minority sports official)	10
Heath	20	Wooller (UK do.)	8
Archbishop of Canterbury	18	Stewart (Labour Foreign Minister)	8
Griffiths (MCC)	15	Helen Suzman*	8
Wilson	12	Lord Boyle	6
Hume	11	Healey	6
Callaghan	11	Maudling†	6
		Ali Bacher (white minority cricket captain)	6

(Total = 203 (38 per cent) of appearances)

*At the time, lone MP of the Anglo-American Corporation's Progressive Party.

†One of the five Heath Cabinet members in 1970 with business interests in South Africa.

The only black person among these leading participants is Kenneth Kaunda, President of Zambia. Although his opposition to the racist minority regime in South Africa is certainly vocal, it is incredible that no black South African was called upon to this extent. It is not normal for the Mexican President to be asked his views on Canada, or for the Turkish Premier to be asked his views on Oman, in British TV news. In all only sixteen ordinary Africans from any part of Africa were called upon to speak or were quoted, along with eight African heads of State. Last but not least, there were precisely two individuals – one appearing twice – who represented national liberation movements from the territory ruled by the racist minority regimes. One was from the Pan African Congress, and the other from SWAPO (South West Africa People's Organization), the main liberation organization operating in Namibia (South West Africa).

Given the standard acclaim in Britain for the heroism and patriotism of French, German and Italian resistance fighters who used violence and terrorism against the Nazi occupying power, this virtual absence of black liberation movement spokesmen from the screen at a period when the region was the focus of unusual public interest, lays television news and current affairs editors open to the charges of active racism or of being politically manipulated. There are so many South African exiles in London and Britain who could easily have been called upon to participate, but were not called, that their absence was either a continuing oversight or deliberate policy.

If it was the first, then it represents the racism of neglect: the assumption that you do not need to ask blacks their views on matters vitally affecting them. This is quite possibly true of the newsroom: Europeans there as much as anywhere else are prone to accept apartheid as less horrifying than Nazism because it is directed against blacks. Such subconscious neglect is active racism because it excludes certain people from speaking about their major concerns when this courtesy would usually be extended to animal-lovers and many other trivial interests.

D

The alternative is that the absence of black spokesmen represents British policy at the highest level of the State. An important clue to this policy is to be seen in the published regret of the Foreign Office in late summer 1973 at its *mistake* in renewing the British passport of the Vice-President of ZAPU (Zimbabwe African People's Union), specifically because he advocated armed struggle for the liberation of Zimbabwe. Many other members of ZAPU and ZANU (Zimbabwe African National Union) have had their passports cancelled. The British capitalist interests involved in the whole of southern Africa are so strong, and are so well represented in the councils of State, that faced with the choice between Mr Vorster and the liberation movements they will surely prefer Mr Vorster, Major Swanepoel, mass starvation policies ('resettlement' in the 'homelands'[3]), the annexation of Namibia, pass-laws and 100 more Sharpevilles (particularly if news about them could be suppressed). They are committed to one side; it is probably the case that through them basic editorial policy in the TV organizations is committed to one side; and so it is presumably hoped that solidarity in Britain with liberation struggles in southern Africa will not take root any further than they have.

For the absence of black spokesmen could only undervalue the significance of the liberation struggle against white minority rule. This meant that the efforts of black South Africans to solve their own problems were played down, that the minor concessions policy of the white political opposition in South Africa was supported,[4] that apartheid was presented as being much less utterly violent than it is, and therefore that a contribution was made to prolonging the present fierce oppression there.

Zimbabwe and its coverage

Both the historical links between Britain and Zimbabwe, and the media coverage of Zimbabwe, provide a close parallel with the case of South Africa.[5] Cecil Rhodes' South Africa Company invaded Mashona and Matabele territory from

1890. The white settlers in its wake were grasping and violent, pursuing forced labour policies and generally behaving as white colonists are wont. Even Milner, then British colonial governor of South Africa, recognized these settlers as the prime instigators of the ferocious counter-attack launched by the proud and organized Matabele and Mashona peoples in 1896–97.

In turn this uprising led to a barbarous pogrom in which superior European weaponry as usual determined the eventual outcome. These years were a bloodbath which at one and the same time showed Africans that the settlers would never compromise about power, and also determined the whites in their conviction that self-rule was essential to them. Any form of restraint from outside by the British government – anxious at that time not to be classed publicly with the atrocities of Belgian rule in the Congo – was an interference they could not brook. They were on the spot, and would keep the blacks down by any means necessary.

It is this colony, numbering in 1974 toward $5\frac{1}{2}$ million blacks and under a quarter of a million whites, with the land divided 50:50 and African majority rule rejected root and branch by the ruling minority, that constitutes Zimbabwe. When the whites seized power in 1965 the British government's reaction was notably muted. Negotiation after negotiation was set up, concession after concession to white racism was offered and spurned – just as in the period 1902–11 in South Africa. Also, just as in South Africa, black deputations visited London in the mistaken hope that Britain would intervene against the settlers. All public appeals, including these deputations, failed.

The contrast with the bloody repression of independence struggles in Aden at the same time, and in so many other colonies where blacks demanded self-rule, clearly demonstrates the official racism of successive British governments.

Inside Britain itself, it was yet another encouragement given to racist beliefs and perspectives. The Labour government firmly displaced the whole question of the demand for liberation by the majority, on to the insult offered the Queen by the unconstitutional UDI. Justice was painted out by legalism.

The economic sanctions instituted by the Labour government have made the economy more self-sufficient and so the Smith regime stronger, have driven the region into still closer union with South Africa, and have presented some whites there with the chance to display their ingenuity at evading them. West Germany and Japan have repeatedly disregarded sanctions anyway, and Nixon excepted chrome – the key Zimbabwean mineral at present – from the USA's adherence to the policy.

It had been hoped by capitalist interests that the fiction of a pro-African settlement might be engineered, until in late 1971 supposedly happy and peaceful Africans rioted *en masse* against the settlement terms. Meanwhile, liberation fighters pursue their struggle with white might in the eastern and north-eastern part of the country, from a position of much greater strength following the victory in Mozambique. For as in South Africa, the jailing without trial for many years now of black political opponents of the regime leaves no political choice to the nationalists but armed struggle. The numbers of those who would appeal for armed British intervention are now fast diminishing – an advance, since apart from any other consideration, the only such intervention likely to take place would be to protect the settlers against rebellion.

The argument most frequently heard in Britain against crushing the settlers' revolt has been the 'kith-and-kin' view. The implication of the argument is that whatever the whites are doing, they must not be treated as outside the international white community. There are two comments which must be made on this angle of vision.

The first is that it directly attacks any international solidarity of class or oppression, and replaces it with a nonexistent white 'community' stretching across time and frontiers. Inside Britain, this idea supports an alliance of wealthy and poor whites, against the minority of blacks. White workers are encouraged by this perspective on the world to identify upwards instead of sideways. A small push perhaps, but a push all the same.

The second comment is that ironic light is shed on the settlers' own claim to be the outpost of European civilization by the many they thought most truly appropriate to be first President of their new republic, Clifford Dupont. Twenty years before, he had been an obscure backstreet lawyer who migrated from London to Zimbabwe in the hope of more lucrative pastures.

The story is all too familiar in British colonial history that nothings became something in the colonies; yet it is a community of such undistinguished people that cannot cede self-government to the 'backward' Africans, and which is treated with such exaggerated caution by the normally punitive British colonial government.

Yet so far as the British news media are concerned, it is this community which *is* Zimbabwe. The very continuation by the media and political leaders of the term 'Rhodesia' aptly symbolizes the basic continuity of white British perspectives and the ways the two countries have maintained their mutual interpenetration over this century. (As in the case of South Africa, one significant index of this interpenetration is the fact that British people are *still* migrating to Zimbabwe.)

Another significant index of continuity is the TV non-utilization of black spokesmen. In 1970 there were 61 news items and 6 documentary or current affairs items, with 130 statements or quotations between them. Forty-nine individuals, groups or institutions were involved. The breakdown was as follows.

White minority government	34 (Smith 25)
British Conservative Party	33 (Heath 14, Hume 9)
British Labour Party	29 (Stewart 9, Wilson 6)
White opposition in Zimbabwe ('Right + 'Left')	16
General unclassifiable	10
Black opposition in Zimbabwe	8
	130

Once again, the South African pattern repeats itself. Blacks although in the majority by far are virtually off the map. No one needs to ask their views, since there are always whites to ask. Once again representatives of national liberation movements are avoided, for whichever reason: precisely two spoke, and that in a single late-night documentary. All in all, concrete data are certainly provided by this survey to prove the accusation by Peter Hain and others that when British newsmen think of South Africa or Zimbabwe they think only of the whites. *The whites alone matter; their reactions to British policies alone count; their opposition is alone interesting; their untroubled survival is alone of concern.* This understanding of the world can only support a racist understanding of themselves by white British workers: by definition, *class* consciousness is correspondingly constricted and starved.

Nigeria and its coverage

The case of Nigeria[6] is particularly interesting after these instances from southern Africa. Although penetrated in the same fashion as Zimbabwe by company rule and the missionaries, followed by the Union Jack, and although the same mixture of guile and violence established the British flag, there was never the same quantity of white settlers as in southern Africa. Also, Nigeria has always been vastly more populous, accounting today for towards a quarter of the population of Africa. Its period under formal colonial rule came to an end in 1960.

Economically, Nigeria is among the top ten oil-producing nations; Shell-BP, 49 per cent owned by the UK government, had £250 millions invested there in 1967. Another £150 millions was invested there by British capital – notably Unilever and the leading banks – at that time in other branches of the Nigerian economy. Britain was also Nigeria's major trading partner at the outbreak of the Civil War. When Dean Rusk, then US Secretary of State, said in 1967, 'We regard Nigeria as part of Britain's sphere of influence',[7] he was therefore both speaking the truth, and signing over responsibility for ensuring an appropriate end to the civil war to British neo-imperialism.

Much has been written about the mechanisms of neo-imperialism/neo-colonialism, whether economic, political, military or cultural.[8] Nigeria is one instance of all these mechanisms at work, the most important for present purposes being the utilization of the division of the country between North and South (*not* the Ibo East and Yoruba West). British colonial policy always held the two regions together despite their salient dissimilarity in most respects, and systematically gave political weight to the semi-feudal North against the South right up to and including the independence Constitution. It is this fissure in Nigerian society which since formal independence has been at the heart of many of Nigeria's problems – not least the civil war itself. The more pre-occupied this leading African country is with its internal problems, the less energy it is likely to have in facing up to neo-imperialism.

British public opinion is, unsurprisingly, poorly informed and misinformed about the structure and mechanisms of neo-imperialism. What therefore happens is that the concrete and specific problems of ex-colonial states, usually inherited from colonial policy as in Nigeria's case, are unknown or dis-regarded. Instead Africans are equated with blacks every-where and at all times, and are judged unworthy of the independence that the whites graciously, generously, and as it turns out unwisely, bestowed upon them! This is not intended to offer an alternative picture of universally noble Africans struggling with an inherited octopus – Nigeria is a class society of a particular, complex kind, and its problems arise also from that fact. The shape they take however is dictated to an alarming extent by colonial history and neo-imperialist activity. Neither the national nor the international class mechanisms are presented by British TV and press; instead, Nigeria's problems and its civil war are interpreted as evidence for blacks' inhumanity, subhumanity, and straight incapacity to manage their own affairs decently. Let us see how.

In 1970 the coverage of Nigeria showed a peculiar feature.

It was allocated an almost identical number of items to Zimbabwe: 77 news bulletin items (Z = 83) and 13 documentary or current affairs items (Z = 6). The amount of *time* allotted was, however, radically different: over $6\frac{1}{2}$ hours of news time (Z = 99 minutes) and practically four hours of current affairs time (Z = 110 minutes). The average length of a news bulletin item, too, was $5\frac{1}{4}$ minutes – between a sixth and a quarter of each bulletin in which Nigeria was presented, which is astonishingly high.

The greater part of this substantial coverage – 70 out of 90 items – was concentrated in a single period of a month, from 7 January to 6 February. In terms of time-allocation, 84 per cent of the total was concentrated in an inner period of just nineteen days, from 12 January to 30 January. Eleven out of thirteen current affairs items also went on the air during this shorter period.

The reason, of course, was that this period marked the end of the civil war and the initial relief and reconstruction programme after hostilities had ceased. The predominant motif of this coverage of Nigeria on British TV was the conviction that something must be done urgently to relieve starvation and deprivation in Iboland since the (black) government was intentionally or carelessly uninterested in the question.

Before chiming in with instinctive sympathy with the humanitarian concerns of television news editors, it is as well to pause to consider a statement by a TV journalist with substantial experience in foreign reporting. In an interview with this writer he noted drily that journalists in that position get to know what the office likes; the editors

like disasters wherever they occur; they like particularly wars showing that anyone whose skin is not white is capable of irretrievable savagery.

Certainly the coverage of the Nigerian civil war and its aftermath was very much an echo of the Congo, *cause célèbre* of the claim that Africans cannot govern themselves.[9] A European civil war between imperialist powers, as in 1914 and

again in 1939, always has real reasons behind it to make it
worthwhile, in the racist view of the world. Civil wars in the
Third World, by contrast, are about nothing, and exist as
evidence for their protagonists' lack of civilization! The kind
of coverage the aftermath of the Nigerian civil war received
reflected therefore the *policy* of TV editors, which was, in turn,
predicated on a racist understanding of the social origins of
civil strife.

So the squads of journalists dashed in to Nigeria, uttered
their dire warnings of starvation into TV cameras for about
three weeks, and then – maybe having purged their emotions a
little – headed out for pastures new. The criticism is not that
they criticized, or drew attention to the disruption of the civil
war; it is that the intensity of their concern was so sudden and
short-lived. White British workers were left with one more
apparent piece of evidence of the 'irretrievable savagery' of
blacks towards each other. The more extreme British racists
were left with another excuse to vent their hostility against
blacks, on the ground that white racists here were not actually
killing blacks or proposing they should be killed – merely
that they should be deported *en masse*. . . .

An instance of the journalists' approach was the way they
commented bitingly on a feast laid on by one military governor
while within fifty miles Ibo children were dying of starvation.
Where, by contrast, were the scorching exposés of continuing
starvation and malnutrition inside the USA, the wealthiest
country in the world? Where were the savage indictments of the
'resettlement' policies in South Africa, which brought *continuing* near-starvation to a million or more South Africans?
Where then were the ferocious investigations of starvation
wages paid by British firms in South Africa, Hong Kong, Sri
Lanka, Malaysia, and many other areas of beneficent,
munificent British investment in the Third World? Where were
the damning surveys of hypothermia in Britain,[10] of accidents
at work,[11] of the impact of large-scale unemployment?[12]

On the one side, continuing policy; on the other the ravages
of civil war. The first does not excuse the second; but the
contrast between British TV's silence on continuing policies,

and its noise on the Nigerian civil war, shows its policy on the latter to have been at best hypocritical, at worst racist.

As regards the people on whom British TV called to speak in this rapid burst of concern, the contours were as follows. One hundred and eleven individuals, groups or institutions participated, on a total of 243 occasions. Thirty-seven black people were called upon to speak or were quoted on 107 occasions. Double the number – 74 – of whites were called upon in this way, although they were allotted only 10 per cent more of the opportunities than the black participants. Of the eight leading participants, four were black (Gowon 29, Effiong 10, Ojukwu 8, Enahoro 6) and four white (Lord Hunt 15, Wilson 12, and the pro- and anti-Biafra MP's Fraser and Foley 6 each). Given that Nigeria is a black African country, the reality of continuing white capitalist domination over it received an unexpected reflection in this heavy representation of white opinion on African affairs.

However, in this instance the journalists from British TV cannot be regarded – as they would claim they ought to be regarded – as outside the divide. Nearly all of them adopted a vigorously interventionist role, attacking the Federal government in detail for the hunger and suffering they filmed. They completely underestimated the resources of the land outside centres such as Owerri in providing basic nutrition. They also left out of account – except in one *24 Hours* item – any reasons the Federal Nigerian government might have for wishing to control relief and reconstruction itself, rather than leaving it to the missionaries and relief agencies.

The relief agencies and the Catholic Church were seen by the Nigerian government as having lent massive support to Biafran claims that genocide was part of their anti-Biafra policy. The Pope himself had gone on record as saying genocide was a possibility. By this and other means these bodies were seen as having prolonged the war and so increased loss of life and consequent bitterness. For example, relief planes were repeatedly used by the Biafrans as cover for much more intensive arms flights. If then any basis for reconciliation were to be laid, it was vital the Federal Nigerian government should be seen to be responsible for relief and reconstruction.

Clearly, therefore, white journalists should be included in the tally of white opinion on the Nigerian civil war.

As regards positions on the conflict, which crossed skin-colour and nationality lines,* there was virtual parity in terms of the occasions on which either side was represented. There were, however, nearly twice as many pro-Biafran as anti-Biafran speakers (64 : 34), which may have increased the impression of opposition to Nigerian government policies. This is rendered even more likely when it is taken into account that the pro-government statements were rarely in the form of detailed justifications for their actions, whereas very detailed attacks were being launched all the time on the Government, with film and pictures to 'support' the attacks.

This failure to present the real factors at the heart of the civil war can only have refertilized the white British worker's stereotypes of African barbarism and brutality. In turn, given the tendency in racist thinking to fuse all blacks into a single entity, irrespective of nationality or culture, this stereotype could only help to block the readiness of many white workers to sense real solidarity with black workers inside Britain itself.

In conclusion then: the use of speakers in the presentation of South Africa, Zimbabwe and Nigeria represents firstly a conviction among British TV news editors and current affairs editors that white opinion is worth infinitely more than black opinion. It revealed, secondly, their opposition to the proper use of nationalist spokesmen for the colonized peoples of southern Africa.

This is despite the increasing utilization by TV organizations of 'experts' – either their own staff who are supposed to develop particular areas of specialism such as foreign affairs

*If to some readers this fact is felt to negate the relevance of the criterion of *black* participation, at the very least in discussions of racism and Third World affairs, then let the reason for the criterion be restated. Whites in Nigeria are a tiny – if privileged – minority. Knowledge about Nigerian affairs is more likely by far to come from speaking with Nigerians, and of France from French people, and so on. British TV operates in the reverse direction, and systematically.

(= the rest of the world apart from Britain and the USA), or university academics invited to pronounce wisely on the topic in question. The expertise of people actually on the receiving end of oppression in assessing what that oppression means, is obviously written off as hopeless bias by the TV editors. The use of 'experts' is in practice an effort to meet the justifiable charge that TV news explains nothing, while making sure that the explanations offered are as bland and inoffensive as lack of explanation.

Not only then is this censorship stimulated in general by the interests of the dominant classes in 'order' and 'stability', but in turn it becomes one element in slowing the development of the class struggle. It is therefore a class operation in both these ways. Naturally the impact of these presentations on the consciousness of white workers and others in Britain is unlikely to be successfully tapped by the crude instruments of opinion-polls and attitude-tests. TV output is a continuing daily and yearly process, feeding the framework of people's consciousness and their taken-for-granted view of the world and their own place in that world. The fact that its output at this point directly parallels the deep-rooted cultural stereotypes of black incapacity and insignificance, and of white ability and importance, means that those understandings and definitions of everyday life are given fresh currency. Whether British workers are to be involved in the struggle against racism inside Britain itself, or against colonialism and neo-imperialism in Africa, depends critically on the currency of these ideas and understandings. A whites-only debate can only sustain them.

If black voices are not heard, especially the voices of the most politically conscious, then the white racist case wins by default. It becomes a frame of mind that white workers are increasingly likely to take for granted, since the only opposition to racism they ever hear much of is also white – and that opposition is very rarely equipped with anything approaching the experience and instincts of the oppressed. Naturally, the perspectives of the oppressed will vary too; and the 1971–72 media-prominence given to Bishop Muzorewa in Zimbabwe illustrated the way a very cautious opposition is typically built up by the media into a very militant one. By contrast, the liberation fighters are kept more or less off the 'map' except insofar as their encounters with Zimbabwe's settlers and their police force are noted from time to time. Any interviews are normally held with the settlers.

Without the growth of political awareness of the threat to their concerns that imperialism and racism pose, white workers in Britain are completely unequipped to develop their own class interests beyond a purely economic struggle. Indeed, the reverse may happen: they may become sucked in, in increasing numbers, to the ruling class's argument about whether Africans and blacks generally are best left to their own devices as in Nigeria, or efficiently suppressed as in southern Africa. In turn, this will impact immediately on the situation of black workers in Britain; and even more explicitly than at present, white workers will allow themselves to be co-opted as agents of repression of blacks, urging their repatriation, the refusal of their rights to jobs and shelter, and maybe even commending the police force for its violence against them. They will tend to identify upwards rather than across.

The coverage of racism in Britain

From examining these critical linkages between Africa and Britain, attention will now be focused on the coverage of racism inside Britain itself. The material will be subdivided into (a) the general contours, (b) the extent to which black people were involved when TV presented something vitally affecting them, and (c) the contrast with the utilization of people such as Wilson, Powell or Hogg, by white interviewers.

At the outset it needs to be stressed that only news and current affairs are under review. Major questions are outside this scope, such as the utilization of black people in the ordinary run of TV programmes, either as people with a special knowledge of the programme-topic, or as featuring in light entertainment, or as actors in plays and serials. However, it should not be overlooked that in broadcasting organizations there is a special relationship between the news and current affairs departments, and much of the rest of the organization. What is happening (as defined by the news departments) has its own forms of influence on themes in both comedy and drama. What is being examined here has therefore a very significant bearing on how black participants are used and abused in other forms of TV output.

The coverage of British racism in the sample accounted for nearly $4\frac{1}{2}$ hours' news time, and nearly $9\frac{3}{4}$ hours in current affairs and documentary programmes. Two hundred and thirty-one individuals, groups or institutions participated directly or by quotation, on a total of 392 occasions. Of the total of participants, 158 (68 per cent) were white, and whites accounted for 296 (75 per cent) of the statements. If black people involved in the 'race relations industry'[13] are excluded so as to check out the number of ordinary blacks involved, the percentage of black participants falls to 28 per cent, and the times they spoke or were quoted to 21 per cent. Already the familiar 'African' pattern is clear, that TV news and allied units normally avoid asking black people their views on white racism.

Discussion of the subject was dominated (40 per cent) by government Ministers and MPs. Since Parliament had distinguished itself by its racist immigration laws since 1962, culminating at that point in the rush law against British Asians in East Africa in 1968,[14] most of these ladies and gentlemen could hardly claim disinterest or freedom from racist views. Other noticeable participants were the police (31 individuals on 34 occasions) and race-industry members (27 individuals on 39 occasions). Even in this professional race-group, the ratio of black speakers to white was 7 : 20, and of black programme-appearances to white, 11 : 28!

Individuals who dominated the debate were Powell (26), Heath (19), Wilson (19), Callaghan (15), Thorpe (10), Byers (8), Healey (7), Hogg (5), accounting for two-thirds of the parliamentary appearances, and over 25 per cent of the total. Clearly, therefore, this was a whites-only debate in essence, as also a dominant class debate. To a large extent also it was a Powell debate: not only did he score more appearances than anyone else, but many of the other appearances were comments on him, thus according him a very considerable place in the sun of publicity.

As regards the contours of the *topics* dealt with, Powell, Powellism and black immigration – all of which are closely associated in most people's minds in the UK – accounted for 51 per cent of the items on racism.* What might be called the Establishment view of racism accounted for 15 per cent of the items. For instance, items on the Race Relations Board; the black comedian Kenny Lynch being awarded an OBE; the Conservative Housing Minister, Peter Walker, expressing his shock at finding thirty-two black tenants cramped inside a seven-room Brixton house (news!); and last but not least, a fifty-minute documentary on the plight of nurses which managed neither to quote any black nurses nor to refer to the racist personnel policies in major UK teaching hospitals. As regards other questions, there were twelve items on Black Power, ten on the police and blacks, and twenty-one others which in some way endeavoured to approach the reality of white racism. All these accounted for forty-three items in all, or about 16 per cent of the total output. I have excluded from this last total the casual verbal pontifications of politicians about racism. There were no items at all about the impact of racism on the position of white workers.

These last items on racism represent a critical test case for the operation of the British TV news media, for small as they

*In case readers may query the categorization of 'immigration' items with racism, it needs to be borne constantly in mind that immigration-laws have been developed to check *black* immigration – the very word 'immigrant' is a euphemism for 'black', as discussions of 'immigrant babies born here' show. In turn these laws have deepened the penetration of racial explanations of scarcity attributing the increase in scarcity to the arrival of black immigrants – scarcity of housing in urban areas, for instance. The focus on 'immigration' has been racist in nature, and so items on 'immigration' *are* items on racism quite simply because they are grounded and framed on racist assumptions. They are racist accounts of racism, disguised as balanced reporting of 'immigration'.

were in relation to the whole output, maybe at least it can be said they grasped the nettle firmly. Before this question is answered one way or the other, however, it is essential to drive home once again the political significance of the gigantic weight allocated to black immigration and to Powell. This concentration helps to lock white workers' awareness of black people on to the very moment of their entrance to Britain, so that it is their colour and 'foreign-ness' and problem-status that *makes* them, not the fact that their labour is exploited too, or that they cannot get proper places to live either, or that they are worried about prices, or that they are worried about their kids, or that they have a sense of humour. This concentration also harps on what black workers are doing to whites as such by entering Britain, rather than on the impact of white racism on black workers (and white workers).

It is a concentration which flows from the insistence of the British state since 1962 that racism is something created by black entry to Britain. The fact that it is a tenacious set of ideas and beliefs already alive and well in British culture, stimulated by the competition within the working class for scarce resources that is the mark of every capitalist society, is not something which the ruling class is usually eager to explain. Instead, laws are passed to stop black entry.

The law, the media, the political parties and Powell therefore mesh and powerfully reinforce British racism. No media editor or reporter then should be surprised at the level of racist consciousness in Britain. What they might do is to ponder the parallel between Powell and – not Mosley, not Joseph Chamberlain, not Nazism, but – Joseph McCarthy, the Red-persecuting American Senator of the early 50s. Here are the astonishingly apposite words of an American political scientist on McCarthy:

. . . though they feared him, it was not intimidation that caused the press to serve as the instrument for McCarthy's rise. Rather it was the inherent vulnerabilities – the frozen patterns of the press – which McCarthy discovered and played upon with such skill. 'Straight' news, the absolute commandment of most mass media journalism, had become a straitjacket to crush the initiative and independence of the reporter. . . . McCarthyism demonstrated that public opinion when incessantly nagged by the instantaneous communications of the mass media and prodded by the pollsters is not capable of rendering sure verdicts on matters of great complexity. Rather it is a bastardisation of the democratic process to imagine that what catches the public interest because it is repeatedly and distractingly called to its attention must be considered the mandate of the public will.[15]

This verdict receives confirmation from an eminent American historian:[16]

He had a diabolical fascination and an almost hypnotic power over news-hungry reporters. They were somehow reluctantly grateful to him for turning out their product. . . . Many hated him; all helped him. They were victims of what one of them called 'their indiscriminate objectivity'.

It may also be noted that the damage that McCarthyism caused within the United States was not ended with his death in 1954; Powellism is equally capable of outliving Powell himself. Powellism is a way of interpreting the world which can absorb new happenings and slot them into its explanatory framework, and which whatever else happens isolates black people from the mass of British workers and offers them as an easy cause of white frustrations and a proper target for white hostility. White British journalists bear a heavy responsibility for failing to expose Powell: not his statistics, but the class enmity of his economic, racial and political policies.

The forty-three items on major issues in the sample were on the following topics. Racism in employment, housing and education totalled ten items, three of them current affairs items. There were seven items on physical violence directed against blacks (one current affairs). There were two on whites' experience of being defined as black (one current affairs). The two topics of the police and Black Power accounted for twenty-two, as noted above; and the remaining two programmes covered West Indians' experience of Britain, and racial friction in Islington, London.

Employment, education and housing are three critical problems for all workers, but even more so for black workers.

To these key questions this 75 per cent sample of British TV news output over 1970 only registered presentations amounting to *eight minutes* of news bulletins, and forty-five minutes of current affairs discussion. There was exactly one item on housing, which was a news item on the difficulties experienced by black students in finding lodgings. Two black students spoke on this item.

There were three news bulletin items on 3 February on a Government White Paper[17] on the employment difficulties of black school-leavers. Here, the only people to be asked their views at all were the police in *News At Ten*! However, in a *24 Hours* programme on blacks in work (10 March) the Indian-born director of a race-relations research organization was called upon to speak, as were some black workers. Another *24 Hours* programme later in the year focused on covert discrimination by a chain of employment agencies in London; here two black former employees of the chain were part of the discussion.

As regards education, only in one *Panorama* item on integration in British education were Asian and West Indian parents called upon to speak along with white parents. The three other items, in news bulletins, covered black children in schools. One person only was asked to speak in one of them, the head of Birmingham's education committee. He illustrated perfectly one of the dominant definitions of black people: as *problem*. Commenting on the fact that there were more black children in Birmingham schools than forecast, he said he did not see why Birmingham ratepayers 'should have to bear the brunt of the problem'. It was, he stated, 'a national, and not merely a local problem'. The only form of participation offered black people in news bulletins about schools was to be dismissively referred to as a national problem. This was at a time when black children were being unloaded in droves into ESN schools and streams, and tossed out semi-literate on to the job market, *because* the educational apparatus was only concerned with how blacks adapted to it, rather than with its obligation to serve all its pupils properly. Given the class nature of the educational apparatus, and the racist bias among teachers and in textbooks, the experience of black children has been extreme, predictable, and disregarded by the media.[18]

When the subject of Black Power arose – a confused concept in many people's minds, meaning often to whites their domination by blacks in the same style currently practised by whites against blacks, and so the subject of some real fear – it was handled in the following ways. There was one item on a Black Panther demonstration in Grosvenor Square, and three of a black protest in Marlborough Street court. No black people were asked their views. Two items on a black demonstration at Caledonian Road police station in London were without black comment; a white journalist was interviewed in one of them. Michael Abdul Malik, self-proclaimed Black Power leader, was interviewed once in a programme all to himself. He was also twice referred to in news bulletins – once as having been arrested, once as having proclaimed he was divesting himself of all responsibilities in the Black Power movement!

The remaining three items on Black Power were extremely absorbing from the point of analysing the ways the news media operate in relation to black people, and especially to black protest. BBC TV News took with the most intense seriousness the claims of a Manchester West Indian to be a colonel in the Black Power movement, and to have discovered a loophole in electoral law which would enable him to flood Manchester City Corporation with Black Power advocates. Enos Beech, the West Indian concerned, was twice interviewed, and said that he hoped to extend this ploy to other cities, and that Manchester was just the first 'to come under the hammer'. In fact, Beech's ridiculous waffle had been prompted by a Mosleyite fascist acting as *agent provocateur*.[19] Later in the year, the whole affair was exposed by a *24 Hours* item; the news sections, however, maintained a stony silence in the face of their own gullibility.

Nothing could have signalled more forcefully the alienation of TV News and Current Affairs editors and staff from black people in Britain than their concentration on the spectacular and absurd, as against their avoidance of black demonstrators with a real grievance about housing or the police or jobs or schools. The notion of Malik and Beech as the voice of authentic and militant black protest no doubt seemed luscious to the newsroom; what it transmitted to white workers, some of them hypnotized by powellism, lasted well beyond the point at which it had passed out of their and the newsroom's immediate memory. What it transmitted was surely the irrelevant fatuity and arrogance of black protest; and which of *them* could get on the box by talking crap like that? The feelings of actively militant black workers were, of course, neither recorded nor canvassed.

The question of the police is an extremely live one for black people in Britain.[20] What happened then in the ten items on this subject? The news items covered black recruitment into the police force, relations between blacks and the police in Birmingham, and a brief report on the exhumation of the body of David Oluwale – a prime example of racist persecution by the Leeds police.[21] Speakers included the police, and a white sociologist who had written a book on the Birmingham police and racism. On two news bulletins, black sixth formers (rare enough in their way) who had been shown round New Scotland Yard were then wheeled out for the TV cameras. There were also two *Man Alive* programmes on the police (13 and 20 May) which included discussion on this topic, a *This Week* which followed the Caledonian Road police station demonstration (referred to above), and a *Panorama* item on the subject. In each of these there were black people involved, though, of course, not to the exclusion of whites. Analysis of each programme would take too long; and so it must simply be recorded that while this black participation was far higher than usual in such programmes, the exaggerated respect for the police, characteristic especially of the bourgeois and petit bourgeois classes in Britain, would require masses of minutely detailed and documented and carefully presented evidence, to be shaken. Further, there are subtle ways of controlling black media participation even when this is permitted; some examples are offered elsewhere in this book. Were blacks to be offered much more access than at present, these subtle ways of control would be much more intensively utilized than thay are at present.

On the subject of physical violence by extreme racist whites against black people – apart from at the hands of the police – the dominant issue was 'Paki-bashing'. (That is, if four news items and one documentary over the year's sample render an issue dominant!) Pakistanis and other black workers were asked to speak in all five items, though it is interesting that one of the five items (26 May) was about the *fear* that Pakistanis might organize to defend themselves and not leave it to the police. Having lived in a part of east London where this violence was fairly common from 1965–69, I can recall vividly the lack of interest among the police in 1967–68 when Pakistanis (Bangladeshis) urged their protection against such attacks. The essence of the police reply was that they could not be everywhere – a reply which itself implied a certain recognition that attacks were frequent.

The other two items were on BBC TV News on 30 December and covered the case of a black family in the middle-class South Coast town of Folkestone. In their Christmas time mail they had been sent a bomb which had it exploded would have killed them all instantly. They were not quoted; but in the *same* news bulletin the director of the National Portrait Gallery was interviewed about the prospects for a national appeal to buy a Velasquez painting (which otherwise would be taken to the USA by its American buyer).

Nothing out of the way so far; except that the subject of the painting was Velasquez' half-African assistant. The Gallery director expressed his elegantly drawling doubt that a public appeal would work, since with the picture's subject at that point in time, 'it really would be flogging the ultimate dead horse'. The reporter's expression, with amused eyes and mouth, as he turned back to the TV camera straight after these words to return viewers to the studio, could be read that he was expecting the joke to be shared by the white viewers. The casualness with which the penetration of racist views, however elegantly and ironically expressed, and their potential implementation in violent attacks, is viewed in the television newsroom was illustrated by the editorial inclusion of both items in the same bulletin. Just how unfunny racism is was not seen to have any bearing on how funny 'everyone' was expected to find the art bureaucrat's remarks.

Twice in 1970, white individuals experienced what it is like to be black in Britain. One was a *Daily Sketch* reporter who took a drug which for a few weeks darkened her skin; she also dressed in Indian clothes and presented herself as of Indian descent. Her shock and depression at the way even passers-by reacted to her presence was communicated in a short *News At Ten* item (ninety-eight seconds). The other person was a Mr George Tonkin, from Poole in Dorset, whose kidney complaint had darkened his skin. He and his wife were interviewed on *24 Hours*. Both these incidents potentially offered considerable scope for the merciless exposure of shibboleths about British tolerance, decency and fair play; and for white racism to be identified as the problem, not black immigration. No such exposure or identification took place; and the isolated position of these items within the 1970 output once again highlights the newsroom's basic concerns.

The two remaining current affairs programmes (on West Indian views of Britain, and of racial friction in Islington) did utilize black participants. The overall picture is depressingly familiar, however; the utilization of black participants in programmes about racism remains the practice of a tiny fraction of producers/editors. The debate continues on the best colonial model, with the whites doing the talking and the blacks mute. Let no one say the TV arc-lights have set on the British Empire. . . .

How do white interviewers perform?

As a final exercise, the style of questioning adopted by interviewers in confronting well-known exponents of racially selective immigration policies, will be analysed. This exercise will act as an important comparison with the non-utilization of blacks, in that the capacity of the white interviewers reviewed to handle the questions of racism is assessed. The individuals whose interviews will be discussed are Wilson, Hogg and Powell.

Wilson was asked in a *Panorama* interview on January 12th how he would keep 'race' out of the next General Election given the keen interest in the topic in the country. Buried in the question is, of course, a perfect expression of the flavour of bourgeois democratic politics: elections are there to be managed and manipulated; and an issue which has been 'repeatedly and distractingly called to (public) attention' (later) must represent the public's spontaneous interest. Also, the way it has been defined to the public and for the public must necessarily represent the public's authentic understanding of the issue.

Wilson should have been asked to defend his responsibility for repeatedly legitimating 'race' as an issue through his controls over black immigration in 1965 and 1968. His reply to the actual question was that evasion of restrictions and the 'problem' of dependants had been dealt with.* He added that a positive programme of community relations was 'in hand'.[22] The trouble, he stated, without actually naming his targets, was Powell and his allies who were stirring the issue up for their own political ends. He, by contrast, had introduced racist immigration legislation for his own political ends – yet the interviewer was blind to that parallel.

On 8 March in a Sunday programme called *Man in the News* Alastair Burnett (then of the *Economist*) and Paul Johnson (of the *New Statesman*) interviewed Quintin Hogg, subsequently to be appointed Lord Chancellor, and one of the central figures in the Conservative Party for three or more decades. East African Asians were turned to at one stage in

*What he meant was that in the committee stage of the *Immigration Appeals Bill* in May 1969, Callaghan had suddenly introduced a clause forcing dependants and all applicants to apply to their unfriendly local British High Commission for an entry permit, rather than have their relatives do it for them in Britain. This could mean journeys of up to 1000 miles in south Asia, only to find Home Office sponsored bureaucratic tangles on arrival. The numbers of dependants entering dropped magically in the run-up to the 1970 General Election.

the interview, with reference to their restricted admission under the 1968 Act at 1500 heads of household a year. The following exchanges took place; emphases of the participants are italicized, while the writer's emphases are in bold type.

JOHNSON: 'There is one other argument about the East African Asians which I've heard, and which I myself **find impressive,** which is that they are for the most part middle-class people; they are for the most part – they speak good English; they have middle-class habits; quite a lot of them have still got considerable savings; and it is argued that if they were now in here, they would in fact form a leadership for the Asian community over here which at the moment needs reinforcement. Would you accept that this is an argument?'

HOGG: 'It's an argument, I don't think it's a fact. . . . I've never seen any hard evidence that this is a fair description; not that I want to say anything against middle-class people – I'm surprised at *you*, Paul Johnson!'

JOHNSON: 'No, no, no, you miss my point there; the fact is that a very large number of Pakistanis and Indians coming over here have very poor knowledge of the English language and a high percentage – I mean I don't agree with you on your "facts" about this – a high percentage of East African Asians in fact have got middle-class standards of education **and would act as a responsible element in the leadership of Asians over here.** That is my point.'

HOGG: 'Well I'm not sure that this is so. . . . I don't think that an East African Asian will necessarily lead a Pakistani **from wherever they come – from the villages of North-West India and so forth . . .** but it wouldn't alter my view one way or the other. To allow the large number of people in respect of whom we are **at risk** all in like *that* – much as one would like not to devalue the British passport – would I think undermine race relations in this country. **It'd make things much more difficult to control.'**

BURNETT: 'You differ from Mr Enoch Powell on those coloured people who are in this country; but you also approve of some degree of repatriation, voluntary repatriation. **How far do you think that could go? How many people do you have in mind?'**

HOGG: 'I have no numbers in mind at all. What I do think is that if you look at the numbers that are going back now under the government's scheme **they are derisory; that is to say they virtually don't exist at all.'**

BURNETT: 'About a hundred a year.'

HOGG: 'Yes. I call that derisory.'

BURNETT: 'What would **not** be a derisory figure?'

The spectacle of one (leftish) Establishment figure arguing the need for *responsible* middle-class leadership among Asians in Britain, and of another rightist Establishment figure urging Hogg to think precisely and seriously about repatriation, offers a perfect illustration of unconscious racist thinking among interviewers. It was their citizenship rights, denied them in Britain because of their skin-colour, which constituted the issue; not whether their skin-colour could be excused if they would keep the other natives quiet in a form of indirect colonial rule. How too could a repatriation programme, the most racist policy placed on the agenda by Powell, become of such detailed and uncritical interest unless it was being taken as a reasonable proposition by Burnett?

As for Hogg's own expressions – 'at risk', and 'a Pakistani from wherever they come from' – it seems hard to distinguish his views from Powell's except insofar as later in the interview he admitted a shrinking from personal responsibility for overt racial conflict, which he judged a large-scale repatriation programme would generate: 'I couldn't bear to be responsible for that myself.'

His analysis, Wilson's and Powell's, that black people *create* racial conflict, and that the more blacks the more the racial conflict, were and are identical. Exactly the same analysis was characteristic of the British ruling-class debate about the admission of Jewish refugees from Nazi Germany in the 1930s. It could almost be said to be a necessary argument for a capitalist ruling class, since if Jews/Blacks/X's do not cause hostility and conflict, the cause must be found somewhere else. And where else than in competition for scarce jobs, housing, education and other services, within and among the working class? And why are these basic resources so scarce for the majority in an affluent society?

These interviewers were not interested in raising that kind of issue; and naturally there is no guarantee that black interviewers selected by British TV organizations would have raised it either. But at least if there had been one alert black interviewer present, instead of these media-appointed surrogates, Hogg could not have got away with his 'at risk', Johnson with his 'responsible leadership' and Burnett with his numbers game. This appeared less a debate than a collaboration!

A month before this interview, Powell had been on the same programme, with the editor of the *Birmingham Post*, and with Burnett once again. A large proportion of this interview has been reproduced in the appendix to this section of the book, and the reader's attention is directed to that for detailed documentation of the analysis now offered.

This interview demonstrated how Powell is only able to get away with his phantasmagoria because the debate on it is confined to fellow-members of the ruling circles. He committed himself in it to the following statements: that 50 per cent of the black minority in Britain would welcome and utilize a properly funded repatriation scheme; that blacks were as anxious as he claimed whites to be about the future increase in the black population of Britain; that the views of a High Court judge, and his own claim of about fifty to sixty letters from West Indians, were solid ground on which to base his own claim to speak for (a) all West Indians and (b) all Pakistanis, Sikhs and Indians, whom he admitted not having heard from personally *despite* there being a large number of Asians in his Wolverhampton constituency! What an imagination! Further, he loosely compared the black population with a typhoid epidemic; he claimed parliamentary uniqueness in being 'driven right up against' the realities, so that his analysis and policy must be justified beyond doubt; he analysed opposition to his views as based on fear of his predictions; and he irrelevantly assured viewers that *he* only found 2–3 per cent of his correspondence on this subject objectionable. Not *one* of these statements was questioned.

Instead, Burnett and Hopkinson produced a series of very open-ended questions which simply allowed Powell to restate his views publicly and defend himself against the most predictable liberal attacks. There was no forthright demonstration of the real impact of Powell's propaganda, merely a series of general accusations without substantiation.

The reason is simple: each one of his interviewers was talking entirely in the dark about black opinion and reactions to Powell among workers. He, however, was prepared to come out with the big bluff, shouting where his argument was flimsy – for instance his repetition of the word 'typical' as he transformed fifty to sixty letters from West Indians into the standard views of $1\frac{1}{2}$ million black people. His interviewers, however, had no basis on which to challenge him. Everyone watching would probably know that however few letters Powell had received, however 'vanishingly tiny' *his* contact with black people, his interviewers would have had still less. At one point postbags on the subject of blacks were compared, Powell's and Hopkinson's, and the latter noted that the people who wrote to him expressed the most disgusting racialism. Here reality was compared to reality; but then Hopkinson shied away from ramming home his argument, even rushing to agree – 'Sure, sure' – with Powell, who absurdly claimed the contents of his postbag were different from the contents of anyone else's. Typically for a representative of ruling circles, all that Burnett could quote substantially against Powell was elite opinion: 'Are you simply a greatly misunderstood man by the majority of the press of this country, by the television of this country, by your own party, by the opposition political parties in this country?' As further evidence for their remote class-based view Hopkinson's statement that black people were delighted to find themselves in substandard accommodation, and Burnett's pitying reference to them as 'quite simple people', were very revealing.

Only an attack on Powell which severs itself from every one of these assumptions, stated or covert, has any prospect of unmasking his propaganda for what it is. Only an attack which relies on accurate analysis of the roots of racism in Britain's imperialist development, in capitalist scarcity, in the pressures to opportunism in bourgeois political parties, and which – crucially – comes from politically conscious members of the black minority instead of media hacks, has any chance of exposing powellism for what it is: a critical danger to all workers, white and black.

As is obvious from the figures quoted earlier, Powell is like a sore tooth to the media; indeed, the more he attacks them, the more their representatives in dealing with him tend to lean over backwards to try to avert his accusations of bias. (They could, of course, fall right over without its changing his stance!) An illustration – the last – of this tendency at work was seen on 10 March, when Powell publicly disputed the Registrar General's statistics of black birth-rates. It is hard to imagine a statistical debate of this kind usually being thought sufficiently gripping to warrant five-and-a-half minutes of news time on BBC2, four-and-two-thirds on BBC1, and six minutes on *News At Ten*. What, of course, made it gripping to the newsmen was that it was a debate about racial hostility, but couched in the racist categories they took for granted.

What stood out about these 'confrontations' was firstly that the interviewers were almost completely uninformed – to them it was just another assignment – and so they provided a perfect foil for Powell to broadcast his propaganda once again. Second, the person chosen to oppose Powell's views on all three bulletins was E. J. B. Rose, a white journalist and director of a fabian study of British 'race relations'. Third, the ground on which Rose attacked Powell was his *figures* – so accepting without question his view that a large number of black people would indeed be disastrous for Britain. The fundamentally racist view that 'immigration "creates" problems' (blacks create racism) was the taken-for-granted framework of this 'confrontation' between Powell and the white media-men.

The conclusion which has to be drawn from this episode as from the others is that there is no answer to Powell for as long as the argument is confined to ruling-class liberals *vs.* ruling-class reactionaries. Powell, like McCarthy, can have it all his own way, dismissing opponents as ignorant or biased, dazzling with statistical virtuosity and apparently 'hard' numbers, and calling for The Great Cleansing Purge of 'voluntary' repatriation. And all this, with the media at his behest for any silly opinion that needs inflating into controversy if it is to survive at all. For the media he has all the hypnotic power of the weasel over the stoat.

Implications for the future

To summarize the material and arguments so far presented: the elements of colonial exploitation and oppression in South Africa and Zimbabwe have been outlined, together with the heavy British involvement in both societies, and the typical media coverage provided by British television. The elements of neo-imperialist domination of Nigeria, the close involvement of Britain, and the coverage of the ending of the civil war by TV, have also been surveyed. The way that Powell and powellite definitions of black workers predominate in TV's handling of domestic racism, the absence of black participants in items affecting them (in Britain as in Africa), the great infrequency with which the realities of white racism were confronted, and the timid weakness and ignorance of TV interviewers facing dominant spokesmen for racist immigration policies, have also been discussed.

What is the significance of this material? Before the final conclusions can be drawn, the impact of the mass media on a modern industrial capitalist society must first be understood. The three critical components of this impact are (a) continuous framework, (b) definition of what is happening locally and internationally, and (c) setting the agenda for public debate and discussion.

The continuous flow of the media is what allows them their capacity to shape people's consciousness: not single startling programmes, but years and decades of varying programmes all predicated on identical or similar assumptions. These keep alive and refertilize the *framework* within which people understand the world and their own place in it. They enable people to draw their own deductions from an event or a development – except that the deductions, while experienced as their own, all too often emerge from systematic frameworks provided over time by the media (and other agencies, such as education).

The definition of what is happening at home, and, of ever increasing importance in today's world, abroad, is the peculiar task of the media. This happens in certain ways in entertainment and drama, but especially importantly in news, current affairs and documentaries on television. It takes place usually within a particular framework, as noted, but has the task of incorporating new developments, on a small or significant scale, into the understanding of the world provided by that framework. If people, especially the working class, are to continue to operate within the existing organization of society, economy and politics, the stability of the definitions offered by the framework in relation to the changes that occur in society is crucial to the dominant classes. From this flows their perpetual anxiety about the content of broadcasting and their nagging concern that it may upset the applecart.

The media set the agenda, less by their direct contact with the millions of individuals who ingest them daily, than by the chains of communication which they set up from parents to children, from friend to friend, and especially by the predominance of ruling-class messages to the subordinate classes. *Who* debates and discusses is therefore of vital significance for the kind of discussion that then takes place. Hence the significance of the yardstick behind the content research on which this section of the book is based: *Who speaks/is quoted, in what role?*

The absence of blacks, especially of politically conscious blacks in Britain or from Africa, from British TV is therefore of decisive importance. *The continuous definitions of what is happening in the world that set the agenda for public discussion and debate are racist.* Not in the straightforward sense that newscasters appeal for violence to be wrought against blacks, but in the much more effective fashion that the violence currently wrought against blacks in Britain and over the world – economic, military, cultural – is out of sight, out of mind. The world that counts is white.

The practical implications of this world-view concern (i) the future of black people in Britain; (ii) the white working class in Britain; and (iii) the future of Britain's relationship with the rest of the world.

(i) Black people in Britain are in a tiny minority, well under 3 per cent of the population. They are exposed to all kinds of insecurity and attacks, even more so than the rest of the working class. In some respects, very much more so. Their future prospects in a situation where militant protest is identified with the late Michael X and Enos Beech, and where otherwise their voice is virtually silent, are appalling. Their current allies are liberals, who by the nature of their strategy can offer no security to them; their potential allies in the working class are currently so politically confused by their history and by the web of pressures acting upon them, that they will often identify as powellism tells them to – upwards instead of sideways. By their operation the media could subvert this consciousness, but as has been shown in practice support it.

(ii) For so long as the white working class rests content with its economism in purely trade union struggles, and with its petty nationalism as a way of understanding its place in the world, it will be more than just a prey to racist appeals. It will also be incapable of overcoming its own exploitation and oppression. It will be unable to understand the possibility of a majority class overthrow of the capitalist economy and of the capitalist state that defends the capitalist economy; or the necessity of this majority class overthrow if the majority is not to continue to be imprisoned in its exploitation. Understanding the possibility may be more of a step than understanding the necessity: people will often tolerate an oppressive situation if there seems to be no way of changing it. The existence of a *mass* revolutionary party is the only avenue to developing this consciousness; in its absence, easier explanations for scarcity and problems are to hand, for instance the blacks. Once again, the media support such explanations; they do not attack them, or enable blacks to attack them, except very rarely indeed.

(iii) The close involvement of British capital in the exploitation of Africans in southern Africa by one mechanism, and in Nigeria by another – there are plenty of other examples – will only be ended by the revolutionary transformation of British society. The future of the British working class therefore has a direct bearing on the ability of British capital to exploit and underdevelop Africa and the Third World. The prospects of *genuine* aid, on the pattern of the Chinese TanZam railway, are entirely remote at present. The media sustain ignorance and misunderstanding of these still-living bonds between Britain and its former colonies; current capitalist relations with the Third World are all the easier to maintain. Even individual exposés such as Adam Raphael's reporting on sub-poverty African wages in South Africa in *The Guardian* in 1973, both remain exceptional at present, and do not call into question the *normal* exploitation of the Third World by British capital – only its most extreme instance.

In the end then, the role of TV in Britain is to be pitted by its historical and structural organizations *against* the basic task facing mankind; a task succinctly defined by W. E. B. Dubois, one of the great black Americans and Africanists of the twentieth century:

The emancipation of man is the emancipation of labour, and the emancipation of labour is the freeing of that basic majority of workers who are yellow, brown and black.

Appendix

Man in the News, Sunday, 8 February 1970 (partial transcript).

BURNETT: 'Now, Mr Powell, what you are saying to the Irishmen who are already in this country is that if you do not accept naturalization as British subjects you cannot vote here, you cannot be a full citizen of this country. That applies perhaps to several hundred thousand Irishmen.'

POWELL: 'I should think so.'

BURNETT: 'Are you not in fact also thinking of something like one million coloured immigrants? Are you not seeking through this device to repatriate white people the compulsory repatriation of many coloured people?'

POWELL: 'Repatriation doesn't enter into this. . . . It seems to me you're rather dragging this other question in.'

BURNETT: 'No, are *you* not in fact responsible for this. Is it not easier to bring about the compulsory repatriation of white people? Do not liberal people accept this because you are not indulging in any racial discrimination on that basis? And can you not under cover of this go about what must have crossed your mind at some time – you have spoken about *voluntary* repatriation – have you never thought of compulsory repatriation?'

POWELL: 'Certainly not. I have always explained that what I was talking about was the policy of the Conservative Party

E

itself* to offer a generous opportunity of repatriation to those who wish it.'

HOPKINSON: '. . . I know that you have never said that you advocated *compulsory* repatriation – I think you've been misunderstood on that point – but do you still feel that a voluntary scheme of repatriation would not be a tremendous incitement to unrest, discord, and increased nervousness among immigrants already here?'

POWELL: **'Oh not at all. The other way round.** You see what the immigrants who are here and mean to stay here and consciously intend to make their homes here are afraid of – **and I know this from those in my own constituency** – are the consequences of the growth in total numbers; and therefore any measures which resulted in those numbers being fewer than they will otherwise be is a reassurance to the immigrants. Over and over again in my own constituency it is the *immigrants* who have come to me and have said, "We are afraid for ourselves unless something is done to stop this continual increase in the prospective numbers" [*sic*]. So I'm in this, as in everything else – I'm acting as I believe and advocating as I believe in their interests as much as anybody else's.'

HOPKINSON: **'Yes, I don't think we would question your sincerity for a moment,** particularly those of us who know you well as a Midlands MP, but I do feel that the number of immigrants who would want to go back on this basis that you put forward would be so small that the numbers one lost from this country would be hardly worth the *political* trouble which the whole thing stirred up.'

POWELL: '. . . From my own experience in a constituency both with West Indians and with *large* numbers of Asian immigrants, and from what little evidence has been delibe-rately collected on this – and I must say I could wish that *more* effort were put into collecting evidence – I believe that

*The perfect neutralization of Burnett, at that time a contender for several Conservative constituency nominations!

this effect would be *very substantial indeed*. Fifty per cent wasn't in fact my own estimate; it happened to be the estimate of **Lord Radcliffe who looked at this independently, and has after all a fairly judicial sort of mind.** So it can't be an *unreasonable* estimate [*sic*], and it does to me correspond with the evidence of my own observation, talking, discussion and correspondence received from immigrants interested in repatriation over the months and years. . . .'

BURNETT: 'Would you still like to be a Minister? **Would you like to be Minister of Repatriation?'**

POWELL: 'If there were a genuine, whole-hearted desire on the part of the administration to *make* such a scheme succeed and to give it the necessary moral as well as financial support, *yes*.'

HOPKINSON: 'Mr Powell, could I ask you? One of the problems as those of us who live in the Midlands* know very well, which we're all concerned about, is not so much the first generation of immigrants, **many of whom find life in substandard houses quite delightful compared with the conditions which they've left in their native land,** but the second generation of **immigrants who have been born and brought up here,** and who regard themselves as Wulfrunians and Brummies and so on – do you feel that these people should be given absolute equality of opportunity with the indigenous English population?'

POWELL: '. . . There's a sentence of mine often quoted as though I'd departed from it. . . . I said I would set my face like flint against any difference being made between two citizens in this country. I say it still, and I've said **nothing** since which **even implies** the opposite. After all, to offer to a man that if he wants to go home you will help him to do so is not discriminating against him!'

*Note the speaker's heavy effort to find common ground and rapport with Powell on the terrain of petty Midlands provincialism, in which he then endeavours to drown black workers' problems.

BURNETT: 'Now, Mr Powell, while you may *say* this, a number of people seem to distrust you when you do say this. A number of people have drawn from your Scarborough speech in which you said that were it not tied to a voluntary repatriation policy which you have just admitted would affect only a very few——'

POWELL: 'I didn't, I believed I had said it would affect up to half of the immigrants.'

BURNETT: 'Up to half of them!'

POWELL: 'Yes. I've just said that. Didn't you hear me?'

BURNETT: 'I didn't *believe* you, Mr Powell, I just——'

POWELL: 'You thought you misheard? Well, let's get it right again: my opinion is that up to half would be, could be **affected** by a voluntary scheme, and I reminded you that this view is not peculiar to me, but this opinion has been stated by West Indians themselves **on the record,** and was the view arrived at by **Lord Radcliffe** – that was how he came into our previous conversation. So I *didn't* say "very few"; and you, if I may say so, are illustrating what I explained a little earlier that it is people who have got it into their heads, though as a matter **purely of prejudice** and **without any investigation,** that voluntary repatriation would affect only a few, who go on *then* to argue that therefore I must be meaning all sorts of things I'm not meaning. Sorry; but I *had* to correct you on that because it's vital.'

BURNETT: 'Well I'm glad to have your assurance of this kind – you think that for £2000 these people would go home?'

POWELL: 'I can produce a great many out of my own files.'

BURNETT: 'How many, Mr Powell?'

POWELL: 'Well obviously from the people who have *written* to me, this only runs into dozens or scores; but as I say, I regard these as instances **which cannot be unique, which are typical – and I use the word again, typical –** of many,

many in similar circumstances. And indeed that sort of evidence really **understates** the readiness of the immigrants as a whole, the readiness of the **whole** immigrant population, because you see almost invariably that sort of evidence comes from West Indians because they speak and write English and are much more conscious of what is being said and offered; whereas the majority of Pakistanis and Sikhs and Indians who would **in my opinion** welcome and accept the possibility of repatriation, are cut off in this country, so that it is unlikely that unless you went below the surface and communicated through their own communities you could find out directly.'*

BURNETT: 'Do you also deny that the purpose of your Scarborough speech in saying that in fact extra help should *not* be given those parts of the country [i.e., where blacks are concentrated] were they not tied in with such a policy, was not in fact meant to put a little bit of a shiver up the spine of some **quite simple people**?'†

POWELL: 'Of **immigrants?**'

BURNETT: 'Yes.'

POWELL: 'Certainly not. . . . The purpose of these grants . . . as your colleague well knows is to prevent the ratepayers and the administration in these particular areas . . . having to carry an absurdly unfair burden themselves. . . . When I said what I said at Scarborough . . . I was not standing up and saying that I objected to a fair deal . . . for the ratepayers of my own constituency.'

HOPKINSON: 'You weren't saying in fact, "Make it uncomfortable for them and they'll go home"?'

*Powell's arrogance in claiming spokesman's rights for black people in this paragraph contradicts directly his refusal to debate racism on *The World This Weekend* with the Revd W. D. Wood in July 1973, on the ground that no single person could speak for blacks in Britain!

†A reference to the Urban Aid Programme, and the Educational Priority Areas policy. Note how Powell ducks out successfully in his next two paragraphs.

POWELL: 'But I've explained that that is not the *purpose* of the grants. . . . If there had been – well, let's take an example – **a typhoid epidemic;** and I'd said, "Well, you know it's no use whatsoever treating the people who go down with typhoid unless we also are doing something about the water supply" – the newspapers the following day wouldn't have come out with headlines, "Powell says: Stop treating typhoid sufferers". Everyone would understand that what I meant was, you've got to take a long view of this thing. And unless you take a view of it on its true dimensions then you are deceiving yourselves and putting off the day when you will have to, by imagining that the **methods of treatment, so to speak, are a false solution.** Of course the parallel isn't meant to be exact. . . .'

BURNETT: 'Are you simply a greatly misunderstood man by the majority of the press of this country, by the television of this country, by your own party, by the opposition political parties of this country?'

POWELL: 'There's very little connection here between the manner in which these subjects are discussed . . . between that atmosphere and the realities as they are known by the citizens of this country.'

BURNETT: 'But who is responsible for this hysteria? Do you damp it *down*?'

POWELL: 'Well, I try to draw people's attention to the facts as I think I see them and the future prospects as I think I see them. And when I do that, people stop their ears, partly for **fear.** Well, I don't blame them – when I look ahead I'm afraid too. And yet I can understand well enough how people who not themselves by their parliamentary situation **driven right up against** these things, I can understand them saying, "Well it'd be more comfortable if I didn't happen to hear that".'

HOPKINSON: 'It is undoubtedly true, Mr Powell, that there would be people who stopped their ears; but my newspaper's postbag reflects invariably after every major pronouncement of yours on immigration an *hysterical* rightist unpleasant upsurge of racialism which is really sometimes quite nauseating to read.'

POWELL: 'Now that's very curious. **I'm not doubting for a moment what you say.** But it is most remarkable how different your postbag then is from mine. This may well be so, because I think that in fact different people write, and write in different ways –'

HOPKINSON: ' – sure, sure – '

POWELL: '– to newspapers or editors from the way in which they write to Members of Parliament. But one of the things which has surprised me – **and I would not have predicted it** – is how tiny, really how **vanishingly tiny** is the proportion of letters that I get which I would class **in any way** as racialist. . . . I wouldn't say that more than 2 per cent or 3 per cent of the total letters which I get on the subject either after a speech or from week to week – because of course it goes *on* – I would regard as **in any way** disreputable or objectionable. So it is *curious*, isn't it?'

NOTES

1. The three major evening news bulletins were analysed on weekdays, together with *Panorama, World in Action, Tuesday Documentary, Late Night Documentary, Man Alive, This Week* and *24 Hours*.

2. H. J. & R. E. Simons, *Class and Colour in South Africa 1850–1950* (Penguin 1969); G. Mbeki, *South Africa: The Peasants' Revolt* (Penguin 1964); R. First (*et al.*), *The South African Connection* (Penguin 1973).

3. C. Desmond, *The Discarded People* (Penguin 1972).

4. Note the prominence afforded Mrs Helen Suzman among speakers.

5. T. O. Ranger, *Revolt in Southern Rhodesia 1896–7* (Heinemann 1967); L. Bowman, *Politics in Rhodesia* (OUP 1974).

6. M. Crowder, *West Africa Under Colonial Rule* (Hutchinson 1968); M. Crowder (ed), *West African Resistance* (Hutchinson 1971), contributions by Smith, Ikime and Muffett; J. Okpaku (ed), *Nigeria: Dilemma of Nationhood* (Westport Publications Ltd 1972); J. de St Jorre, *The Nigerian Civil War* (Hodder & Stoughton 1972); R. First, *The Barrel of a Gun* (Penguin 1972).

7. *West Africa,* 22 July 1967.

8. P. Baran, *The Political Economy of Growth* (Penguin 1972); F. Greene, *The Enemy* (Cape 1970); C. R. Hensman, *Rich Against Poor* (Allen Lane 1971); C. Palloix, *L'Economie Mondiale Capitaliste* (Maspéro, Paris 1972); S. Amin, *L'Accumulation à l'Echelle Mondiale* (Anthropos, Paris 1972); H. Magdoff, *The Age of Imperialism* (Monthly Review Press, New York 1969); R. I. Rhodes (ed), *Imperialism and Underdevelopment* (Monthly Review Press 1970); M. Barratt Brown, *After Imperialism* (Merlin Press 1970); K. Buchanan, *The Geography of Empire* (Spokesman Books 1971); H. Schiller, *Mass Communications and American Empire* (Kelley, New York 1969); R. J. Barnet, *Intervention and Revolution* (Paladin 1972).

9. For more enlightening accounts of the Congo, see T. Kanza, *Conflict in the Congo* (Penguin 1972); and C. Kamitatu, *La Grande Mystification du Congo-Kinshasa* (Maspéro-Belgique 1973) – publication is banned in France.

10. See the articles by R. H. Fox in the *British Medical Journal* for 6 and 7 January 1973.

11. T. Nichols & P. Armstrong, *Safety or Profits* (Falling Wall Press 1973); also the Annual Reports of the Chief Inspector of Factories.

12. G. Standing, 'Hidden Workless', *New Society* (14.10.71), pp. 716–19; T. Gould and J. Kenyon, *Stories from the Dole Queue* (Temple-Smith 1972).

13. J. Downing, 'Britain's race industry: harmony without justice', *Race Today* 4.10 (October 1972), pp. 326–9.

14. D. Steel, *No Entry* (Hurst 1969); and in general, Michael and Ann Dummett, 'The role of government in Britain's racial crisis', in L. Donnelly (ed), *Justice First* (Sheed & Ward 1969).

15. D. Cater, *The Fourth Branch of Government* (Houghton Mifflin Co., Boston, 1959), pp. 73–4.

16. D. Boorstin, *The Image* (Weidenfeld & Nicholson 1966), p. 22.

17. Cmd. 4268; see John Downing and David Wainwright, 'Blasted talent and lumpenproles: what the White Paper didn't say', in *Race Today* 2.4 (April 1970), pp. 120–2.

18. See particularly B. Coard, *How the West Indian Child is made educationally subnormal by the British school system* (New Beacon Books 1971); M. Maxwell, *Violence in the Toilets* (New Beacon Books 1971); F. Glendenning, 'Racial stereotypes in history textbooks', *Race Today* 3.2 (February 1971), pp. 52–4; J. Hill (ed) *Books for Children* (Institute of Race Relations, London, 1971).

19. L. Kushnick, 'Black Power and the media', *Race Today* 2.12 (December 1970).

20. It is the subject of numerous reports; the best single collection is D. Humphry, *Police Power and Black People* (Panther 1972).

21. For an account of how David Oluwale came to Britain an alert young man in the early 50s, and via prisons, mental hospitals and the police, ended up dead, see R. Phillips, 'The death of one lame darkie', *Race Today* 4.1 (January 1972), pp. 16–18.

22. For a thorough analysis of 'community relations' bodies in Britain that entirely refutes Wilson's claim, see M. Hill & R. Issacharoff, *Community Action and Race Relations* (OUP 1972), and I. Katznelson, *Black Men – White Cities* (OUP 1973), Part III.

6. Media and Identity: the Asian Adolescent's Dilemma

Graham Faulkner

The last twenty-five years have seen the rapid growth of the television industry in Britain. This particular medium of mass communication has grown from a position of being a luxury enjoyed by only the rich to an institution that is taken for granted by people in all walks of life. Nearly all families now own a television set or have easy access to one, and the advent of colour transmission, has led to the two- or three-receiver family. With the pervasiveness of television it is perhaps inevitable that people should begin to ask questions about the significant contribution that it was making to our society.

Indeed, such questions have been asked; by academics, by the clergy, by Members of Parliament, by journalists, by television authorities, and eventually by the lay public. The sort of questions asked have generally been concerned about the effect that the content of television programmes has had on the consumers of that content. Unfortunately, despite the simplicity of the questions, and some would argue because of their simplicity, no clear-cut answers have been found. Many of those involved in the debate over whether television causes certain forms of behaviour have argued that elaborate investigation of the issue is unnecessary, that evidence can be found simply from observing the amount of behaviour that is clearly attributable to television. Indeed, the newspapers are quick to report court cases where there is evidence that the stimulus for the crime came from the mass media. The argument among groups such as Mary Whitehouse's National Viewers and Listeners Association is that it is 'commonsense' that television can cause crime (see Whitehouse, 1967). Even

Michael Swann, the Director General of the BBC has argued that the Corporation must assume that there is a causal relationship between media presentations of violence and violence in society. Likewise academic research, and extensive and expensive research at that, has concluded that there is a small positive correlation between viewing violence and television and aggressive behaviour, and that this relationship only occurs in certain people in certain environmental contexts.

I would argue that television's impact is far more subtle than this, and that it is the psychological and social factors that predispose people to this relationship that should form the basis of research. However, studies have often taken random samples and looked for general universal influences, as if all people should be affected in the same way by the same content. Such an approach is unsatisfactory because it masks subtle changes which when summated may cancel each other out, those showing zero effect across the entire sample.

In the past, the evidence quoted for the direct causal relationship between media and other forms of behaviour has been either based on correlational studies, or laboratory work. Neither of these is completely satisfactory. Laboratory studies observe behaviour completely out of its normal context, and assumes that the random selection of samples will provide information related to the general population. They have also focused on short-term effects: does the viewer imitate the behaviour he has observed the next time he is placed in a situation similar to that shown? He might not the first time, but may on subsequent occasions. There are many other criticisms of this type of study, e.g., the social connections of the viewer are ignored, the processes of selective perception are overlooked, etc., and these have been extensively documented elsewhere (see, for example, Klapper (1960), or McQuail (1969)).

The correlational studies are equally inappropriate, the main reason being that one has to infer the direction of the relationship. For example, if it could be shown that two events, A and B, are positively correlated, what can we infer as to the cause and effect? On the data available, it could be that A causes B, that B causes A, that A and B are caused by another event or series of events C, or several other explanations. Why then do people choose to infer a causal relationship from correlational studies between viewing violent television content and aggressive behaviour? The simple answer is that it seems to make sense. It makes more sense (at least to those who argue for such a relationship) to interpret a correlation between the prevalence of violence in the mass media and its prevalence in society as evidence that the media are a major causal factor. Equally a correlation between Bible reading and violence would be interpreted differently, probably in terms of the Bible reading being an attempt to quell the urge to act violently, and that without the Bible, violence would be even more prevalent in society. Statistically, it is equally meaningful to reverse the interpretations and to suggest that people who feel an urge or who have a tendency to act violently turn to television to reduce the urge, and that Bible reading is causally related to the increase in stone throwing at football matches!

Extending this argument to the more general level, it leads us to consider whether television programmes influence the shape of society or whether they merely reflect what is already prevalent. As with nearly all social scientific controversies, the truth probably lies in the compromise of the two extremes. Television programmes both reflect and influence; for plays to be believable when set in modern times they must reflect certain aspects of the society. Equally, it is true that television is one of the major channels for the dissemination of information, and as such shapes certain aspects of society. For any individual member of society, who is also a viewer of television, the function that the media perform for him depends on his social background and psychological makeup. For certain groups, the media do not reflect, they do not show them in their true light. To be black, to be female, or to be of a left-wing political ideology means that the image of you that is presented in the media is inaccurate and lacking in positive associations. Basically the media reflect the official, middle-class, white, Protestant values of British and American society.

For non-whites in Britain, whose culture is markedly different from that of the British middle-class, the mass media are more able to influence than reflect. The picture of the non-white that emerges from television is that of an 'immigrant', a term despised by many blacks who have been born or brought up in Britain, who regard themselves as British and think of Britain as their home. It is still a rare event in this country for a black to appear on television other than as an immigrant, frequently illegal, or else in a discussion on race relations. Such portrayals as do occur tend to be stereotypical. The Indian is a snake-charmer or a bus conductor wearing a turban who eats curry, the West Indian is happy-go-lucky, rhythmically musical and very athletic. These portrayals are often the focus of comedy programmes in which the essence of the jokes lies in their racist implications. When blacks appear in 'serious' programmes, they tend to be culturally British or American. They dress according to Western standards, in short could equally well be played by a white. The only programme currently being produced by BBC or ITV which presents an accurate reflection of Asian value systems and cultures is *Nai Zindagi Naya Jeevan,* a magazine programme specially produced for Asians and screened at 9.00 a.m. on Sundays.

However, whether the correlational evidence is indicative of causal relationships, or whether it merely suggests that the mass media reflect the current state of society, is immaterial. What is more important is that there is a degree of semblance between how things are and how things are depicted to be in the mass media. Television content contains many clues as to the power relationships and the behaviour thought appropriate to different roles within our society. To a native Englishman, born and bred in this country, these background cultural factors will already be well-learned, or at least the vast majority of them will. Scenes of everyday life will seem 'natural' and 'right' to him, so much so that he will often be unaware of the underlying role relationships which are the basis of the realism of the programme. The behaviour shown will seem familiar because he shares the assumptions which form the basis of the behaviour. For example, a woman in the kitchen making a cake or ironing appears quite normal and natural and will give the viewer little cause for concern, however, a man engaged on similar activities will seem unusual and possibly amusing; indeed many comedy programmes are based on such role reversals. In short, the general television fare, based as it is on Western societies, offers, by and large, a familiar picture to the viewer. It is familiar because it is a representation of the society he knows. However, for people brought up in a different cultural setting, or in a vastly different society, the basic assumptions may be very different and the behaviour shown in drama not familiar at all.

It is within this framework that one should consider the media behaviour of Asian children in this country. Their parents have been socialized within societies which make very different demands of young people. Often these differences can be more than one of degree, they can be completely contradictory. For example, in our society young people are free to choose their own mate, and have a considerable degree of freedom in planning their own social lives, and will eventually make a separate life for themselves away from the parental home. For many Asian children, especially girls, many of these basic ways of life, which young people in our society take for granted, are totally forbidden. They have their marriage partner chosen by their family, and to ensure that they get a good match for their daughter, parents supervise her social development closely and allow her little freedom. Dress tends to be more conservative, the diet vegetarian, and the girls are taught home-making, cooking, and sewing from an early age, although they will probably spend the early years of marriage with their in-laws in an extended family group.

These brief outlines of the expectations for young people in the Asian and British cultures are gross over-generalizations. However, they do indicate that what is regarded as 'right' or 'normal' behaviour varies according to the culture within which the observer of the behaviour has spent most of his life. The behaviour that Asian children are confronted with when they watch television or when they read a comic may seem strange and perplexing, just as it seems strange to British people that anyone could derive satisfaction from allowing their parents to choose their husband or wife.

However, before discussing in detail the situation of young Asian children in Britain, it is necessary to introduce a concept from the American literature on media behaviour and some of the related findings concerning non-white audience members. When viewing a television programme, one often becomes involved in what is happening, shutting out external stimuli and feeling that one is 'in the hero's shoes'. This is especially true with children, who can become totally absorbed in a programme and not even respond when their name is called. This feeling of putting oneself in a character's place and experiencing, albeit in a vicarious and second-hand manner, emotions related to the character is known as *identification*. No completely adequate definition of this term exists in the literature, but the general meaning involves the process whereby a viewer feels empathy with a media character, and experiences certain aspects of the content in relation to this character. This definition has been left deliberately broad so as to include the situation of experiencing the same emotions as the character would experience, i.e., to feel fear when he is in danger, and the related situation of imagining oneself to be the object of the character's attention.

Eleanor Maccoby (1957, 1959) and her colleagues suggested that the character chosen for identification will be the one who by his actions most satisfies the needs of the viewer and who is most like him in major social characteristics such as age, sex, and race. These two factors have received empirical support both by Maccoby and by Rosenkrans (1967); however, in both cases the two conditions were complementary. The character most able to satisfy the viewer's needs, usually in terms in information-presentation, was also like him in some social characteristic. What would be the effect on the child's media behaviour if there was no character who was able to satisfy his need who was also like him in social characteristics?

The overwhelming majority of research on the identification and media behaviour of non-whites has been carried out in America on Negroes. Goodman (1952) and Coles (1965), using doll-play and picture-drawing techniques respectively, demonstrated that many Negro children longed to be white and tried frantically to rub the black off their face and hands. They refused to draw anyone they liked as being black and, when asked which doll was like their friend, consistently chose the white ones. Bradley Greenberg, with a team of associates, has conducted a programme of research at Michigan State University on the media behaviour of Negroes, and their identifications with media characters (see Greenberg *et al.,* 1969). He showed that approximately 25 per cent of Negroes identify with at least one white media character, apparently supporting the more general work of Coles and Goodman. Indeed, Greenberg interpreted his results in the same way as they had interpreted theirs, that Negroes wished to rid themselves of their negative racial identity and assume a more positive white one. However, Greenberg failed to explain the high percentage of white subjects who identify with black characters, over 40 per cent in his study! A good deal of the American data which is available on this issue has been produced by Greenberg and his associates, and much of it is unsatisfactory on such grounds. A recent study by Clark (1971) showed no such cross-racial relationships with respect to identification with media characters. The data do not therefore allow a conclusion about which factor is more important in influencing identification, the ability of the character to satisfy the viewer's needs or a degree of similarity between the character and the viewer. Of course, to find a character similar to oneself may be one of the important needs of the viewer, particularly in the situation of an Indian adolescent viewing British television, and thus the two variables become further confused.

What then are the reactions of young non-whites in this country to the type of media fare that they consume? What influence does this media content have on the cultural conflicts that characterize their social development? What are the consequences of observing the power relationships as shown on television; relationships which emphasize that to be white, middle-class, Protestant and male means that one has power, whereas to be black, young, Punjabi, and female means that you don't belong, that you are of low status, and that you should 'go back where you came from'.

From 1971 to 1973 the author has talked with many young Asians about their experiences in this country, and the data that is presented here is based on these discussions and interviews. The impressions that have been formed cannot be statistically assessed, their significance cannot be judged by consulting tables of statistical significance levels. The position of research workers in the eyes of the black community has reached a level where thorough, methodologically-sound, and theoretically sophisticated studies are no longer tolerated, because they are of no value to them and will not help them in any way. The following arguments can be backed only by the author's experience and over fifty hours of taped interviews; if they represent only half the truth they deserve to be taken seriously for their implications are far-reaching. It is all too easy to be complacent about race relations and to argue that eventually things will settle down and that there's nothing really to worry about. There is, at this present moment, a generation of young people growing up in our society who have every right to be here, who were born here in Britain and who know no other country. They will not accept, and we should not expect them to accept, the label of 'immigrant' or 'second class citizen'. The fact that many of these young people are being told that their racial identity is somehow inferior or unsatisfactory, the fact that the culture in which they are growing up may be vastly different from that experienced by their parents in their childhood, and the fact that the mass media seem unwilling to accept that simply because another people's way of life is different does not imply that it is inferior or funny, are issues that must concern us all.

The interviews on which the following observations are based were carried out in seven schools in the East Midlands between June 1971 and July 1972. Several of the interviews were carried out when the India–Pakistan war was at its height and the media coverage was focusing on the plight of refugees and the devastation of the Indian sub-continent. As such, it represents a period in which the amount of time given over to India was disproportionately large. Nevertheless, it is the more mundane and general media content that occupies us here, although the reader should bear in mind this unusually large amount of media time devoted to India.

Television contains a continual stream of information related to how society in Britain is organized and to the features that define the cultures in this country. These cultures, and there are many, related to social class differences, regional differences, and age differences within the general population, although seen as vastly different by the people brought up within them, contain many similarities. Although a Yorkshire farmer, or an Eton schoolboy, or a Welsh miner would see the other two as being completely different from himself, and would also no doubt regard his own life-style with pride and think it superior, there are gross similarities between them all. They would probably all share the same first language (although there would be marked differences in the way they spoke it), they would probably all share the same religion (at least at the most general level of all being nominally Christians), they would eat the same type of food, and wear the same type of clothes, etc. They would have conceptions about the class relationships in this country, about the common family structures and life-cycles. They would all know that one goes to secondary school at eleven or thirteen, that it is unusual to get married before eighteen years of age, that one is able to vote when over eighteen, that one retires at sixty-five, etc. As such their cultures can be regarded as sub-cultures within one broader and more general culture. Their different outlooks on life, their attitudes, values and opinions, are variations on a theme. The larger theme relates to having been born and bred in British society, and being under the initial influence of parents who had already internalized the norms and values of this 'British culture'. It is indeed difficult for readers who have themselves internalized this culture to recognize that such a gross umbrella exists over the diversity and variations between sub-groups within British society.

However, when it is argued that immigrants should become 'integrated', or 'assimilated', it is this general British culture that they are expected to learn and accept. They are expected to follow the general principles of the culture, to wear British clothes, eat British food, and to take their place at the bottom of the British social class system.

The first generation of Asians, the immigrants from India or Pakistan, have usually had no desire to become Anglicized; just as the British settlers in India have remained stoutly British in the way they live, the Indian settlers in Britain have, in the main, established communities which have allowed them to follow their own traditional way of life. The situation is, however, markedly different for their children, often called the 'second generation', who will grow up in this country and therefore be subjected to many influences related to British culture. At school, they will be taught British history, including Britain's glorious empire-building in the Indian sub-continent, and in virtually all subjects implicit references to British culture will be made. They will also mix freely with English children who will pass on cultural information, often in a cruel way. The author heard many tales of Indian girls being made to cry by the ridicule of their English class-mates over their accents, or when they came to school in *shalwars* (the tight Indian trousers, often made of silk), or when they refused to cook meat in domestic science classes. However, the most significant carriers of information about British cultural values, especially for young children, are the mass media, and in particular, television.

Roger Bell (1968) argued that: 'One of the most powerful external influences in any Indian immigrant home is the television, a potent source of conditioning towards the mores of the host society'. Over 90 per cent of all the second-generation Asians spoken to claimed to watch some television every day. As Bell implies, television is able to convey information about the norms of British society, even if the child does not intend to learn anything from viewing. This is not to claim any form of subconscious process of indoctrination, simply that the relationships between people and the ways they behave towards each other recur time and again. The behaviour expected of people in different relationships are repeatedly defined in dramatic programmes. These relationships may very well be unimportant as far as the story is concerned, but they may be the major element which makes it realistic. As argued above, they are taken for granted by people who have already learned the subtle rules governing these relationships, by people who know the sort of behaviour that is appropriate between say children and their parents, or between customers and shop-keepers, etc. However, for second-generation Asian children, who may not have learned these relationships, television is a potential source of information and learning. It is less demanding than learning through social interaction, where one runs the risk of being ridiculed if one does not know the 'correct' way to behave.

One of the most consistent themes that appears when Asian children talk about television is that it offers them a chance to learn English. Language is central to any culture, and television allows children to listen in on other people's conversations without being thought impolite. It carries information about the types of speech that are appropriate in different situations. To a child living in an environment where no one speaks English, as is often the case in an Indian home, there is no other alternative if he wants to learn the basic means of communicating with people in the British culture. Until he has learned at least some English he can master little of British culture.

When they first arrived in England, many Indian children knew little or no English, and were faced with a strange country in which they were unable to communicate with the vast majority of people. Stories of arriving late at night, being cold and frightened, and not understanding what was happening, were common. Frequently they were followed by stories of gradually learning English from watching television. In these early weeks and months in this country many children said they never went outside the front doors of their houses, and spent virtually all their time either reading or watching television. When their parents had occasion to leave the home, to look for work or to buy food, they were often struck by the immodesty of the dress of English people and the overtly sexual contacts between men and women. In Indian cultures, it is thought improper for a husband to touch his wife at all in public. These impressions cause them to discourage their children from going into what they consider to be a decadent society. The following comments, made by some twelve year old Gujarati and Punjabi girls, are typical of the reactions of Indians when first arriving in Britain:

TV is good for us, when they speak English, we can learn the language more.

I couldn't speak English when I first came, my dad taught me and I learned from television.

My only hobby is watching television. In the summer holidays I just sit in the house and watch TV.

Mum couldn't speak English so we told her to watch television and now she can understand a bit.

Crossroads helps me to understand by saying all sorts of words that I don't know.

Although this appears to be the initial way in which the children, and to a certain extent their parents, use television for information about British culture, it is unlikely that it will be an enduring function. Indeed once they start school English will be their main language of communication for a large part of their day, and special lessons are often organized by the school if a child's standard of English inhibits normal teaching. It should also be borne in mind that television was only used as a supplement to language learning, none of the children interviewed said that they had relied totally on television. However, the *Sun* of 8 March reported the case of a girl who had come to Britain from the south of France and had learned all of her English from the television programme *Till Death Us Do Part*. She later had to have corrective language lessons because of the excessively coarse nature of her speech!

The language problem is likely to be greater for children

who have come to this country direct from India. However, a large proportion of Indians in this country have either come from one of the East African countries, often as a result of forced expulsion due to Africanization programmes in those countries, or else have been born in this country. For these children, English may well be spoken in the home, at least by their father if not by both parents. Although this would seem to make the transition into British society easier, it has often had the opposite effect. Their lack of verbal fluency in English, their strong accents, and the considerable differences in climate and way of life between Britain and East Africa have often led to a situation known as 'culture shock'. Children mentioned the speed at which life was lived in this country compared to the more relaxed pace in Tanzania or Zambia, others spoke of being able to go to the beach every day at home and wondering where the beach was in their new industrial home town, and one girl said she preferred Africa to Britain because she 'didn't have to stay in all the time and watch television there'.

Children who react in this way are thought to suffer when first attending school. Bernard Coard (1971), a West Indian educationalist, lists culture shock as one of the main reasons that a disproportionately large number of West Indian children are classified as educationally subnormal. The classification is, he claims, often made on the basis of IQ tests and other measures taken before the children have fully adapted to their new environment. Many of the children that I interviewed reported feeling shy or scared when they first went to school, so much so that they preferred to stay at home and watch television. They withdrew from personal contacts or else spent their time with other Asian children who were new to the school even though they could not talk to them in many instances. Several friendship groups were found where all the members had a different first language. These children very rarely had any contacts with people of their own age outside school, and spent their lesure time working, on domestic chores or at school work, or else watching television. The following comments are typical of such children:

I was puzzled when I first came and when I saw all the public and the traffic and the ladies riding bicycles, it was pretty odd to me. When I first came to school I had no friends, I felt shy and I didn't know how to make friends. I wondered if anyone would talk to me and I was scared.

It was horrible when I first came to school here. I couldn't speak English and I was scared and shy.

It was awful when I first came. Dad kept telling me to speak English but I couldn't and I was very shy.

These same children show a strong liking for certain types of television programmes, programmes which they claim help them to understand people. The actual programmes chosen as favourites for this reason varied greatly, from *Startrek* to *Blue Peter*, from *Crossroads* to *Alias Smith and Jones*. People in these programmes were often described as 'friendly' or 'kind' and one girl said that she liked the people in *Blue Peter* because they showed her 'how to get on with people'. However, despite the traumas of these early years, it is the later years and the experiences with the mass media when settled at school and fully conversant with the language that appear the most significant. The overwhelming popularity of the mass media, and in particular television and comics, among Indian children is striking.

Asian girls are, by tradition, the bearers of the cultural norms. It is the women who are entrusted with the job of maintaining religious observation within the family, and of passing the traditional norms and values on to the younger generations. That girls adhere to traditional ways is seen as being vitally important to the preservation of Indian cultures in Britain. They are expected to live a reserved and restricted life, to eventually accept a marriage arranged for them by their family, and to then build a family adhering to traditional mores. The Women's Liberation Movement in Britain represents the very antithesis of the traditional way of life thought appropriate for women in Indian society.

Whilst it is true that many Indian families who have emigrated to Britain have become westernized in their outlooks, and have now accepted that the extended family, whereby all generations of a family life together is impractical in a 'two-up, two-down' terraced house, the position of women is one of the more resilient areas of Indian culture. The problems that these pressures cause for any Indian girl in Britain will vary greatly and will depend on how she reacts to the thought of an arranged marriage, of not being allowed to go out with boys, and of not being able to wear the clothes currently in fashion. She will also have to face the fact that when leaving school she will be expected to marry straight away and not take a job.

When first attending secondary school, where there are older girls who dress and behave in ways which are totally alien to traditional Asian cultures, these pressures will be brought to a head. Added to these, the mass media play a major part in defining the behaviour appropriate for young people in our society. They provide both first and second generation Indians with a picture of what is and what is not expected of young people in British society. How the second generation Asian girl reacts to the conflicting models of youth that are presented to her by her parents and by the mass media and possibly older girls at school will set the basis of her later social development.

The age of eleven to thirteen appears to be the crucial period of development for Asian girls, mainly because it is the period when they first come into regular contact with other English girls with whom they could identify. It also represents the period of their lives when they begin to be judged within the British educational system in a more demanding environment than they will have encountered at junior school. This age has been shown to be important with respect to media behaviour. Collins (1970) showed that at this age the ratio of the learning of background information to the learning of central information in a film was at its greatest. That is children aged eleven to thirteen were likely to remember more of the background or non-essential information in any film in relation to information that is essential to the plot, than are either older or younger children. The sort of information labelled as 'non-essential' by Collins consisted of the type of information regarded here as implicitly culturally related. For example, the type of clothes worn by certain characters, the type of food they eat, how they speak to their parents, all of this information will be generally unrelated to the plot of the programme, it is often the touches of realism that are included to make the story believable. Therefore, Asian girls, who have reported watching television in order to learn about people, would be most likely to gain this information at the age eleven or thirteen, namely when they are first attending secondary school.

The interviews provide ample evidence of the conflicts between parents' and children's attitudes, and in many cases it is clear that the mass media are intensifying these conflicts. Television in particular sets expectations and aspirations that are totally unacceptable to the traditionally-minded of the Asian community. One Indian girl claimed: 'I'd like to go to clubs like they show on *Top of the Pops* when I'm older, but I don't think I will because of my parents'; another talked of her ambition to get an 'interesting and exciting' job when leaving school: 'I like the dancers on *Top of the Pops*, called Pan's People. I'd like to be a dancer when I grow up,' and many other girls had similar job aspirations. Nearly all their plans were related to things they had seen on television, and few accepted the possibility of an arranged marriage and no job: 'I don't want to get married, none of the Indian girls do because it's just like the old days, our parents choose our husbands.'

A vital factor in intensifying such conflicts is that of the relative authority of the parents. Within the Asian cultures, authority is based on age. The oldest male member of a family is regarded as the authority figure in that family. It is his will that sets the limits of what is acceptable behaviour for the younger generations. This was especially true in the extended family in India. In Britain, television can act as another form of authority; its message can be accepted or rejected, but it cannot be directly questioned.

Many teachers spoke of the difficulty in teaching subjects when there had been a programme on television on the same subject; for if the information that they presented in a lesson was different from that shown on television, the television was quoted by children as the ultimate authority. At the time of the interviewing, the series *The Seven Wives of Henry VIII* had just finished, and several teachers talked about children quoting minute factual details from these programmes as evidence that their school textbooks were wrong. Some children even argued that the pictures in the books didn't look like the wives really were, because they had seen them on television. This was found to be the case with English as well as Indian children, all accepted the authority of television in areas where they had no first-hand information.

English children were quick to make comments about other countries, and when asked to justify what they had said, the most common comment was that they had *seen* it on television. Words could be untrue, but pictures couldn't lie. The power of the visual element in television should not be regarded lightly, to children of eleven and twelve, seeing is believing. That is, except in areas where their first-hand experience tells them otherwise. For example, again drawing on the discussions with English children, many thought that the programme *A Man Called Ironside* was unrealistic. Their reasoning was that they had come into contact with policemen and they (i.e., the authorities) would not allow a man in a wheel-chair to be in the police force. Similarly, programmes like *Please Sir!* and the *Fenn Street Gang* were thought far-fetched because 'the teachers wouldn't let you get away with that sort of thing'. *Skippy* was thought to be an accurate reflection of life in Australia, and perceptions of other countries were often based exclusively on television programmes about them, irrespective of the time-setting of the programme.

For children of non-English cultural backgrounds, the vast majority of television content is based on the culturally unfamiliar and is therefore likely to be believed to be accurate. Conversely, they do not believe the programmes which are based on or set in countries which they have lived in before coming to Britain. One Kenyan Asian girl said that: 'People in Kenya aren't like they show on television, they don't live in the jungle. It's just like it is here, except that the houses have got flat roofs.'

Thus the behaviour of young people, or of people in certain occupations, is regarded as normative when presented on television, and the life-styles, which are often glamourized for television, are thought commonplace. Parents of Asian children also see the behaviour of young people in British society as shown on television and regard it as typical. Thus the conflict is intensified, the children want to be like their English peers at school, to be one of the gang. To be accepted they must dress in the accepted way, which means following the fashions. They must also listen to the latest pop records, and be able to talk about them. Increasingly they will be expected to go out with boys, to be concerned about cosmetics and to go on social outings with friends from school. These are all seen by the parents as signs that their daughters are rejecting the Indian culture. The parents have formed impressions of British society from personal contacts and also from television, and often they regard it as decadent and immoral. Thus, the gap between parents and children is increased by television; it presents a life-style that is highly desirable for the children but highly undesirable to their parents.

English children, as well as Asian children, reported that their parents imposed restrictions on their viewing. For English children the restrictions were in the form of sanctions against watching certain types of programmes, most often the late night horror films and programmes thought to be sexually overly explicit. On the other hand, Asian parents stopped their children watching television *per se,* and irrespective of the content. Frequently they said that it interfered with their children's school work or damaged their eyesight. 'My brother watches *On the Buses*, but my parents don't like it. It's the way they are civilized, they don't like the things we do. Dad is not too keen on television at all.'

Apart from intensifying conflicts between the culturally defined life-styles of young people, television also implicitly defines the characteristics thought beautiful in British society. In terms of Collins' work, the actual physical appearance of the heroine in a play is usually classed as 'non-essential' information, however certain physical characteristics recur in women called 'attractive', 'beautiful' and 'worthy of the hero's affection'.

These physical characteristics vary greatly, but almost always the heroine is white. What will be the reactions of non-whites in the audience, how will they reconcile the fact that they do not possess the major defining feature of beauty, namely a white skin? Which characters will the Indian girls identify with, given that the appearance of an Asian woman as a heroine on British television is indeed a rare event?

In general the people admired on television, the people they would like to be like, varied greatly. Often pop-singers were mentioned, with Lulu and Olivia Newton-John being the most popular. However, choices weren't limited to women; Cliff Richard, Elvis Presley and David Cassidy all were mentioned frequently. Several of the Negro men characters who appear regularly were also well-liked: Mark in *A Man Called Ironside*, Morris in *Mission Impossible* and 'that Negro (coloured) man in *Love Thy Neighbour*'. But when describing these characters, children assiduously avoided mentioning skin colour, and very few felt able to talk about skin colour at all. One girl who liked the programme *Julia* described the leading character (Dihane Carrol) as being 'just a little bit black'.

The portrayal of whiteness as being associated with beauty and goodness was clearly understood by children of eleven and twelve. They were also able to generalize the definitions of blackness implicit in media content, making negative references to dark men, or the cowboy in the black hat. They also seemed to link blackness with dirtiness when talking about the countries from which they had come and evaluated this blackness negatively. The sun was often blamed for making people black. For example:

I don't want to go to India because you get sunburnt there and I'm already brown enough and I don't want to get any worse.

I didn't like India, the people are all dirty.

I didn't like Nairobi much, there were too many black men there.

These and similar comments also indicate that the children evaluate their own racial identity negatively. A few children even claimed that their family had moved from Leeds, or Bradford, or London because there were too many Indians there! Of course, the intensity of prejudice and discrimination directed towards Asian communities in such areas may well have provided a powerful motive for leaving. But the fact remains that it was their ethnic identity and their skin colour which brought down on them the hostility and rejection of the white, host community.

Those children who accepted that they were Indian, and felt pride in their racial identity, often looked to adult Indian figures for their models. An admired uncle or a successful grand-parent, often only known to the child through the tales told by his parents, were envied and the child set his sights at emulating them. There were, however, a considerable number of Indians who were strongly identifying with their own cultural heritage, but could find no adequate adult model within that culture. The parents were not admired, possibly because they had not done well since coming to Britain or because they had abandoned some aspects of the culture, and the mass media provided no ready substitute. Two of the schools visited had Indian teachers and they were greatly admired by a small proportion of the Indian children who showed other signs of still adhering very strongly to Indian customs. These same children reported staying up very late at night, an unusual occurrence normally, to watch the news reports from India.

However, in general, Asian children who valued their racial cultural identity were dissatisfied with their school curriculum and with the content of television programmes, for the same reasons, namely no recognition of their cultural background. One Indian girl criticized her history lessons bitterly. She had come to England from Tanzania and said, 'I know a lot about African history, now I'm learning English history, but I don't know anything about India.'

Others complained about the timing of *Nai Zindagi Naya Jeevan* which is shown early on Sunday mornings, and many children wished that there were more such programmes. Indeed it does seem unusual that the television companies have not seen fit to cater more for what must be regarded as an eager and captive audience. It is estimated that over 80 per cent of the Asians in this country listen to the BBC's present broadcasts for Asians (Hiro, 1971) and the undoubted success of the weekend showings of Indian films at local cinemas are surely indicators of a need for Asian-based mass entertainment.

The Indian films, to which the traditionally-minded regularly take their children even when they are in a language that the children cannot understand, seem strangely paradoxical. The parents see them as representations of their culture, even if it is a glossy and over-produced representation, and yet their content often highlights one of the parts of the culture most sensitive to Western influences. They reinforce the Asian cultural elements through their language, usually Hindi but occasionally Gujarati or Punjabi, and through the style of dress worn, the type of food eaten, and most of all the abundance of popular sitar music. And yet, the themes are often of romantic love, and of the struggle of a daughter to escape her parents' attempts to force her into an arranged marriage when she has fallen in love with someone else. There are often long drawn-out family feuds and it is not uncommon for the audience's sympathy to lie with the heroine who eventually wins and marries the boy she loves.

The romance in these films is well veiled, there is little or no physical contact shown on the screen, and kissing is strictly forbidden. Indeed it is over romantic or sexually permissive television content that Indian children most often reported conflict with their parents. Many say that British television is 'too sexy', that their parents forbid them to watch *Top of the Pops* because the dancers 'don't wear proper clothes'. Comics such as *Jackie*, and to a lesser extent *Bunty* and *Mandy*, which contains stories of the 'boy meets girl' type were extremely popular but often hidden from parents. The problem page of *Jackie*, in which readers write in with beauty problems and for advice about their boyfriends, was one of the most popular parts of the British mass media with Asian girls.

However, of all the ways that the mass media tend to highlight and intensify cultural conflicts perhaps their most important function with regard to Indian teenage girls is in providing them with information about how to get on in British society. Many children report liking a variety of different programmes because they show them what their own lives would be like when older or because they showed them how to get on with other people. Ambitions for jobs tended to be high, and often they planned to go and live in America or Canada when working. Their conceptions of what working life in these countries would be like were usually fanciful and far-removed from the truth. One girl even said that she wanted to go to America to live, but was a bit nervous about all the cowboys there.

Whether or not these ambitions are merely the pipe-dreams of young children or whether they represent genuine desires for greater freedom than is customary within the Asian cultures is unclear. However, there are strong indications that already conflicts of wishes are developing between first and second generations. The children cannot write to their families back in India, as their parents would wish, because they cannot write in Punjabi or Gujarati, and their relations cannot read English. The children are beginning to regard the life-style defined for them by their parents as old-fashioned and too restrictive. The life-style they see as a replacement has been largely fashioned out of vague impressions formed from television programmes. Whilst it is no doubt true that all children go through a stage of wanting to be train drivers or nurses, the consequences are more severe for Asian youngsters. Often a family will totally disown a child for being seen with a boy or for wearing short skirts. The desire for freedom from the cultural restrictions can therefore, if only representative of a temporary stage of development in our culture, mean severe problems for a traditionally-minded Asian family.

The second generation Asian children in Britain, those

born or brought up in this country, no longer think of themselves as Indian or Pakistani. They think of themselves as British, think of Britain as their home and expect the same opportunities as are made available to native-born British youngsters. They reject their own racial identity, often speaking about the 'immigrants', the 'blacks' and even the 'Indians' in derogatory terms. They feel proud when Britain does well, they support the English football teams, and they want to achieve success and status within British culture. Their parents may want to return to India, but the thought of leaving Britain is a frightening one to the second generation,

England's my home now, and I find it hard to make and keep Indian friends.

I don't want to go to India, I've got used to it here and I've been brought up here, I'm just like the English girls now really.

I like it when they put up new houses, you feel proud when you see a new building in (this city).

They accept British standards, British values, and aspire to jobs which carry high status within British society; in short they regard themselves as culturally British.

When they grow up, they find that this society defines them as immigrants or Indians or blacks, or other terms which they have learned to associate with low status positions. They have learned these relative status positions, in part, by seeing them repeated in television programmes. The life styles which they have seen to be the most desirable in these programmes are reserved for the English/people. They will come to realize that they are excluded from full participation within the society with which they identify. By this time, they may well have moved so far away from the Asian culture that they are no longer acceptable within this culture, they cannot find refuge among the Asian community. They will become a rootless generation with no social anchoring points. The mass media have been an important factor in producing disillusionment with the Asian way of life, and expectations of something better from British society. But it is British society, which remains unwilling to accept a black face as being worthy of equality, which must ultimately carry the responsibility for the future of the growing number of dissatisfied black British youngsters.

NOTES

R. Bell (1968), 'The Indian Background', in R. Oakley (ed) *New Backgrounds: the immigrant child at home and at school,* Oxford University Press for Institute of Race Relations, 1970 (2nd Edition), pp. 51–69.

C. Clark (1971), 'Race, identification, and television violence', in G. Comstock, E. Rubenstein, and J. Murray (eds), *Television and Social Behaviour,* Volume 5 of a technical report to the Surgeon General's Scientific Advisory Committee on Television and Social Behaviour; U.S. Government Printing Office, Washington, 1971, pp. 120–84.

B. Coard (1971), *How the West Indian Child is Made Educationally Subnormal by the British School System*: New Beacon Books for the Caribbean Education and Community Workers' Association, London.

R. Coles (1965), *Children of Crisis*: Faber and Faber.

M. E. Goodman (1952), *Race Awareness in Young Children*: Collier, New York, USA.

B. S. Greenberg *et al.* (1969), '*The Mitchigan State University CUP Reports on Communication*': A mimeographed series of research reports.

D. Hiro (1971), *Black British, White British*: Eyre and Spottiswoode.

J. T. Klapper (1960), *The Effects of Mass Communication*: Free Press, New York, USA.

E. E. Maccoby and C. W. Wilson (1957), 'Identifiable and observational learning from films', *Journal of Abnormal and Social Psychology, 55*, pp. 76–87.

E. E. Maccoby, C. W. Wilson and J. Burton (1958), 'Differential movie-viewing behaviour of male and female viewers': *Journal of Personality, 26*, 259–67.

D. McQuail (1969), *Towards a Sociology of Mass Communications*: Collier-Macmillan.

M. Rosenkrans (1967), 'Imitation in children as a function of perceived similarity to a social model and vicarious reinforcement'; *Journal of Personality and Social Psychology, 7*, pp. 307–15.

W. A. Collins (1970), 'Learning of media content: a development study': *Child Development, 41*, pp. 1133–42.

M. Whitehouse (1967), *Cleaning Up TV: From protest to participation*: Blandford Press.

F

PART IV

In this section three journalists provide contributions derived from their own particular experience in working in the British news media and reporting race relations. Lionel Morrison is a black journalist who as a freelance has covered race relations at home and abroad. His personal experience of working in Fleet Street provides a particularly powerful indictment of the British press. Derek Humphry writes from a different perspective as a staff reporter on the *Sunday Times*, he has for some time had a particular interest in race relations, and rare in journalism, has had time to research his stories. Alexander Kirby as editor of *Race Today*, the monthly magazine of the Institute of Race Relations, was able to experience the superficiality of tolerance, and expose hidden interests, when his magazine challenged white interpretations of race relations and sought to make known the black experience of life in Britain. These contributions from within the journalistic profession indicate how various are the pressures, from outright job discrimination and financial leverage to the everyday routines of journalism, which make responsible reporting of race relations so difficult to achieve.

7. A Black Journalist's Experience of British Journalism

Lionel Morrison

One autumn morning in early November 1968, I had an appointment at the editorial offices of a liberal daily morning paper. The appointment had been arranged a few days earlier, after I had made enquiries about a possible subbing vacancy on the paper. I had been asked by the then night editor either to contact him or the chief sub.

I announced my presence that morning to the receptionist who then duly informed the night editor. He said he would come to see me.

After about ten minutes, a gentleman emerged from one of the sections on the floor, came down the foyer, passed me and the receptionist at her desk and peered around looking for someone. Not finding who he was looking for, he then approached the receptionist and asked her where Mr Morrison was, as he could not see him. The receptionist had the grace to blush and pointed at me. The gentleman did not blush, introduced himself as the night editor and invited me to an office for a talk where the chief sub would join us.

As I got up to follow him, I pondered the problems of having a Scottish surname and an 'unblack' accent, and of not having informed him before that I was a black journalist.

The interview, especially with the chief sub who put me through a thorough interview, was, however, fruitful. Another sub was leaving in two weeks and could I then start? They were happy with my qualifications and experience and wished me to start on the usual three months' probation. They would inform me when exactly to come in. Handshakes all round as

I left, and I was prepared to forget the whole foyer incident. Had I not, after all, got the job? A black journalist, I graciously argued, was the last person the night editor had expected to meet, especially since I had informed him in my letter that I had had newspaper experience in South Africa, Asia, Europe and other parts of Africa, had been to university and had travelled extensively. Experiences expected more from white journalists than black ones.

After two or three weeks there was no communication from the paper, and it was then that I saw an advertisement in the UK Press Gazette for a sub-editor for the same paper, requesting the same qualifications and experience as previously for the same job. Needless to say, I did not apply for the post and have not heard since from either the night editor or the chief sub.

There was and still is no doubt in my mind that I did not get the job precisely because I was black.

When I started applying for jobs in Fleet Street in 1968, after returning to this country from Africa and Asia where I had held senior journalistic posts, I did not for one minute think it would be easy. I knew there was race prejudice in Fleet Street and in the British news media as a whole. But I had hopes of exceptions, like the liberal paper of my memorable experience.

Blacks have been brought up to believe that the British 'liberal' press is the most enlightened, the most concerned and the most sympathetic. But my own experience and that of other black journalists tends to place a doubt on these general attributes. Their news reports speak up strongly against racialism, discrimination and prejudice, but unfortunately that is as far as their liberalism goes. It does not extend inwards into the holy sanctum of the reporters' rooms, where the media image we have of ourselves, whether black or white, is written or broadcast by a pure white hand.

It is this hypocrisy and dichotomy of standpoints on race which is the hallmark of our liberal press in this country. So that the biblical injunction that it would be easier for a camel to squeeze through the eye of a needle than for a rich man to get into the kingdom of God, can aptly be applied to the heavenly world of British journalism, if one interchanged the rich man for a black journalist. Indeed it is so rare to meet a black journalist on British newspapers, TV and radio that the few who are there are real curiosities.

Of the 28 000 journalists working on British newspapers and magazines, less than two dozen (or 0·09 per cent) are black. (Compare this to the country's black population percentage of about 3 per cent.) Most work on the various West Indian and Asian language papers and magazines and the overwhelming majority are unfortunately not trained nor professional in the journalistic sense. The rest, who are professional and experienced, number less than a dozen and work on the hundreds of daily, weekly and monthly British magazines which play such an enormous and vital role in shaping people's community and race relations ideas and actions.

There are two black journalists in training on two newspapers in the country at the moment. One in Bradford and the other on the South East London *Mercury*, whose editor, Roger Norman, is one of the few local newspaper editors who does not hide behind a plethora of excuses like, 'if blacks would only apply', or, 'they don't have the right qualifications'.

In the subbing field there are more at Thomsons and the Westminster Press papers, where they are hidden behind desks away from the public spotlight that accompanies actual reporting. The number of actual frontline black reporters is indeed rare and in Fleet Street I know of only two others, besides myself.

It is quite true that journalistic standards for ordinary entry to the NCTJ (National Council for the Training of Journalists) proficiency certificate scheme have risen and candidates need at least five 'O' levels. And the tendency to go for graduates or 'A' level applicants has also increased. With the educational system as it is presently for black children, the problem becomes understandable. But an obsessive acceptance of this argument was quite rightly slammed by someone very well placed to know what he is talking about.

In a letter to the race relations journal, *Race Today* (September, 1973), Mr J. Clement Jones, CBE, past Editor of the Wolverhampton *Express and Star*, had this to say:

There are now a number of alert young West Indians and Asians who would make every bit as good a showing as some of the white youngsters who offer themselves for selection and subsequent training as journalists. Much of the trouble is that dissuasion for blacks starts well before the selection stage – in fact by school careers masters and youth employment officers.

That the majority of editors who are in the market for trainees certainly are not racist is happily true. But the majority are content to take a passive line and to duck out from underneath, with the familiar formula 'of course, if the right black boy or girl came along, etc. . . .'. And in this way they are aided by the career advisory system, to preserve the *status quo ante immigration* [author's emphasis].

The position on the journalistic side of the communications industry is, however, in advance over the attitude on the printing and associated sides. I have watched black stone-hands and lino-operators working with considerable skill and expertise in their own countries, but there is overt colour prejudice in the print shops of Britain. Moreover, on the commercial side of the communications industry black advertisement representatives are regarded as a grave embarrassment when there has to be face-to-face confrontation at point of sale.

Sadly the race relations industry as a whole has chosen to look the other way when it comes to dealing with the communications industry, out of a sense of fear that if it embarrasses the industry on the equality of employment front, it will itself get inequality of treatment on the publicity front.

And commenting on *Race Today*'s hope that the injunction of the Kerner Commission into Civil Disorders set up by President Johnson to inquire into the race riots in America in 1967, that 'The communications media (in the US), ironically, have failed to communicate and that they have not communicated to the majority of their audience – which is white – a sense of the degradation, misery and helplessness of living in the ghetto', should not come true in Britain, Mr Clement Jones says it is already too late. *'Of course we have failed, because we of the communications industry have never ever really wanted to succeed and consequently never tried'* [author's emphasis].

This serious indictment of the British press, by a respectable former editor of one of the leading provincial papers illustrates the hypocrisy which governs the press's attitude to racialism in theory and fact. It is so much easier to condemn racialism in columns of print, but it is a different matter to do something positive about it, like training and employing black journalists.

My own experience in this field aptly illustrates this point. Between late 1968 and early 1969, after my interview with that liberal Fleet Street paper, I applied for over ninety jobs. Ninety per cent of these were advertised vacancies and the remaining a cross section of Fleet Street papers which I thought or had heard might have a vacancy. Between the two sorts, I virtually covered the whole of Fleet Street except for about three or four papers. The papers covered North, East, West and South England, the Midlands and most of the Greater London papers.

I informed all but ten that I was a black journalist. I got replies from these ten. Three in the provinces offering me a job, the rest had already filled them. Because of the very low salary offered, I did not take any of the three offered jobs.

Of the eighty whom I had informed that I was a black journalist, 45 per cent had the courtesy to reply. Some of those who did not reply went on advertising for the vacancies weeks afterwards.

The standard reply from the 45 per cent (or forty replies) were:

(a) The posts were filled and they thanked me for applying. (Fifteen replies.)

(b) The posts were unfortunately filled, but they were grateful for my interest and would retain my application in their files should a review of the position or another vacancy arise in the future. (Twelve replies.)

(c) They were seeking professionals from UK papers only.

This was not to say they would necessarily exclude journalists from overseas under different circumstances. (Eight replies.)

(d) The vacancies were filled, or they had no vacancies presently, but they would like to meet me. (Five replies.)

In relation to:

(a) Advertisements for the same post in at least half the papers appeared two or three weeks after their replies to me.

(b) None ever contacted me again, in spite of the fact that numerous vacancies appeared in their respective newspapers during the past three years.

(c) White South African, Rhodesian, Australian and New Zealand journalists who had never actually worked on UK papers before got jobs from these papers with no difficulty.

(d) When I went to see those in this category, it was clear that 80 per cent wanted to see me out of sheer curiosity. As one editor remarked to me: 'It is the first time I've had the pleasure of speaking to a coloured journalist who was resident in this country'. The remaining 20 per cent were genuine in their attempts to help me on a freelance basis, as they had no staff jobs available. They included the then editor of *The People*, Mr Bob Edwards (now editor of the *Sunday Mirror*) to whom I owe a lot.

In my quest for a job, the papers I had not approached in Fleet Street included the *Telegraph* and the Beaverbrook Press groups. The reasons were obvious. These papers I had been told and believed were so right-wing, especially as far as race relations reportage was concerned, that for a black journalist even to harbour the thought of contributing to them was a gross sacrilege. As my efforts to get a decent job on any British paper failed one after the other, I decided to go freelance. I took a pot shot at the *Sunday Telegraph* for free-lance assignments. To my surprise I found this paper had none of the hypocrisy which so many Fleet Street papers so vociferously suffer from when it comes to accepting contributions from a black freelance. George Evans, assistant editor of the *Sunday Telegraph* and man in charge of the famous in-depth and investigative 'Close-Up' section of the paper, asked me after a long discussion to help the Close-Up team in some of their investigations. This was the beginning of a fruitful journalistic liaison between me and the *Sunday Telegraph*.

Although I must categorically state that I do not share the paper's general stand on race relations, I would not and have never been asked to write anything on race relations which was against my beliefs.

I also started freelancing with *The People* at about the same time, where I found a similar non-hypocritical atmosphere.

Because of the political and racial atmosphere which then prevailed – powellism was at its height – and the competitive journalistic market, there was no alternative but to specialize in race and community relations even though one resented the Fleet Street assumption that black journalists were only good and expert on reporting exclusively about blacks.

It might be asked why do black journalists accept this situation? The answer can be nothing but a purely pragmatic and non-altruistic one.

Fleet Street is saturated and it is the vogue, whether one likes it or not, for specialization. To make a living it is best for a black journalist, especially where and when there is no encouragement for him to report on general matters, and where in any case he would be trampling on someone else's toes, to capitalize on his position of being black. One can also argue that it is better for a capable and involved black journalist, knowledgeable of the black scene, than a white 'black expert', to report first-hand on blacks in this country.

I think, however, there is a line which black journalists must draw in this argument. If it means being given race relations stories, especially when they are treated on a crisis scale, then no self-respecting black journalist worth his salt should accept such a commission. It is the duty of all journalists, both black and white, as well as editors and broadcasting authorities to make every effort to portray ethnic groups in other than conflict situations. Jamaican-born Barbara Blake, who worked for both Thames and ATV, left and returned to her native country precisely because she felt she was being given race relations stories when they were handled as 'the wogs are making trouble again'.

In deciding to specialize as a black 'black expert', I found no difficulties on certain papers where my special knowledge was welcomed. The problem arose on the so-called liberal papers who had their own white 'black experts', their own race relations experts.

These experts are the ones who have fashioned to a great extent the stand of their various papers on race relations. They are the 'experts' on blacks. They jealously guard their position and resist any newcomers and intruders in the field. They react even more vehemently when the intruders are black. This, no doubt, is a consequence of the old paternalistic doctrine which was and still is so strong among some liberals. They know the black, his desires and shortcomings better than blacks themselves.

Papers like the *Sunday Telegraph,* the *Sunday People,* and the *Evening Standard* are, I found in my experience, the few exceptions in this regard.

The white 'black experts' on the *Sunday Telegraph* were no woolly-footed liberals, nor pretended to be, and in line with earlier observations did not see in me a threat. Instead they welcomed and respected my expertise, and my viewpoint.

A similar atmosphere has prevailed at the *Evening Standard,* a Beaverbrook paper and the evening stablemate of the right-wing *Daily Express.* The *Evening Standard,* to the surprise of the black community, has pioneered reports on blacks by a black journalist himself. Not just the odd feature which is the discerning mark among the 'liberal' papers, but constant, regular reports. There is no doubt that the stand taken by the *Evening Standard* has helped tremendously in introducing a new element in the thorny field of community and race relations as far as Fleet Street is concerned.

Fleet Street on the whole always tends to look for the problems accompanying blacks. Sometimes to such an extent that people start believing that every social and economic problem facing this country is in one way or another there because of the black presence in this country. And worse still, some blacks start to think like that. Fortunately papers like the *Evening Standard*, although not sweeping discussion of grass-roots discontent relating to community and race relations under the carpet, have started to project over the past three years blacks as ordinary people with ordinary desires, fears and ambitions.

There is no doubt that the editor of the *Evening Standard*, Mr Charles Wintour, has committed himself and his paper to this task. It is, therefore, in this light that Mr Wintour's viewpoint that the greatest contribution the media can make to peace and harmony is by the *quietness* with which it speaks, becomes extremely relevant. Continual treatment of racial matters on a crisis scale discourages the view that racial crisis can be avoided. Crisis treatment encourages a crisis attitude.

On 14 August 1970, Richard Crossman, then editor of the *New Statesman*, discussed the clashes between the police and the black community in Notting Hill on 9 August. What he found distressing was the fact that none of Fleet Street had any black reporters on their staff who could report the clashes. The report caused great interest in the black community and I decided to reply to Dick Crossman months later when the *New Statesman* had replied with great gusto to Enoch Powell, after one of his periodic outbursts. The letter challenged the *New Statesman* to do something about the lack of black reporters on its own staff. Because of the pertinence of the issues involved, this letter is reproduced as it essentially reinforces my arguments about the media.

Mr. Richard Crossman
Editor
The New Statesman
Great Turnstile
London WC1V 7HJ   19th February 1971

Dear Mr. Crossman,

For some months I have been hesitating whether I should write you this letter or not. At one time I had persuaded myself that I should forget it all in case it seemed as if I was carrying a chip on my shoulder. But alas, the recent outburst by Mr. Enoch Powell and the predictable response by socialists like yourself and others, reluctantly decided me to write this letter to you and *The Statesman*. I hope it is not too pertinent or bitter. It is just disappointingly angry.

I am coloured and have been a journalist for the past 14 years, having worked in South Africa, Indonesia, China, Vietnam and Zambia as a reporter, newscaster, executive editor of a magazine and sub-editor. I have travelled extensively in nearly all African and Asian countries and can with all modesty and sincerity claim that I am fairly well keyed-up with events in the developing countries. I am presently freelancing in Britain, specialising in race relations.

Having been forced to leave South Africa ten years ago, because of my anti-apartheid views, I came to this country and after a year registered as a British subject. I was proud to become a citizen of this country. But that was ten years ago. I am not so sure whether I am so today.

Racism has popped its ugly head with telling results in this country. Powell I understand and can cope with. But what I can't cope with is the response by his opponents and especially those in Fleet Street. I am not writing about those editors and papers who covertly support Powell. I mean those who oppose him and go so far as to become the advocates of the Black man. They are more soul destroying and in Labour MP Eric Heffer's unparliamentary words 'bloody hypocritical'.

You, Sir, wrote in *The New Statesman* of August 14th, 1970, when you discussed the clashes between the police and the coloured community in Notting Hill on the 9th August, that what was distressing was the fact that none of Fleet Street had any black reporters on their staff. You were dead right.

But unfortunately you did not go further. During that week I was called on by some Fleet Street editors to report on what had happened. Two papers, *The People* and the *Evening Standard* carried articles by me and gave me a by-line stating plainly that I was a coloured reporter and had been living in the area. Now that was a rare thing to do in Fleet Street and I appreciated it. *The People* have subsequently carried articles by me on a freelance basis. This generosity I can only attribute to the sensitive and non-hypocritical attitude of its editor, Bob Edwards. Now and then some other editor has done the same. But only on a freelance basis.

I have written to and made over 50 applications for jobs in the newspaper field in London and the Provinces. Many of them sounded very interested. They were very reasonable in their replies and over the phone. When they actually saw me, they realised they had been carried away by my surname which is as Scottish as roast beef is English. It was then that all professional interest disappeared and sweet reasonable hypocrisy set in.

The first thought I am sure that went through their mind was: Blimey, he is black. What does he know about Britain? And, it would not do for a black man to report on matters which effect black people in this country at all. All these editors have their white 'black experts', whom I am given to understand, know Africa better than the Africans, Asia better than the Asians, black homes better than black men and women, and what it means to be black in a predominantly white society. I have been verbally told time and again that I will not fit in as the particular paper has its own race relations expert who knows everything that is happening in the black world here and abroad.

But worse still. Being black I therefore cannot report on anything that is British and therefore white (an inverse powellism). I do not disagree that Fleet Street is generally saturated, but when you read the *UK Press Gazette*, you are amazed at the number of new appointments which are taking place in Fleet Street and the provinces. It is as difficult for a black journalist to get on to Fleet Street papers as it is for the biblical rich man to get into heaven. I was once told by a black militant that reporting was a 'white concern'.

Yet I know many white South Africans who have migrated to this country, and who have less reporting and journalistic experience, but because (and so I must unfortunately assume) they are white get a job immediately and without difficulty in Fleet Street and on so-called liberal papers.

My worst experience was with a daily liberal paper. I wrote to them, they invited me over for a chat. At the reception I waited for the night editor, who passed me twice and was searching the passage for a Mr. Morrison. White I suppose. He approached his reception and was told that I was the gentleman he was looking for. At that moment I knew I would not get the job. Later, together with the chief sub we had a discussion and I was told emphatically that there would be a vacancy in two weeks' time and that I would be called and given the job on a three month probation period. Needless to say I never got the job. I was never called, but I did see a subsequent advert two weeks after I had applied for the job, for applicants. And that from a paper which writes the most anti-racist leaders and articles and takes a very moral attitude towards injustice.

But, Sir, what about *The New Statesman*? Does it employ any coloured writers on its staff? My experience with *The Statesman* is also not a happy one and has indeed added to my disillusionment. About this time last year I sent two articles to your paper—granted you were not editor then. The first was returned with a note which said that recent events had outstripped the contents. Yet the matter was discussed in the media for another month and was important. The second feature was returned after a month with a terse note that it could not be used, that is after I had been on the phone for more than five times to find out what was happening to it. Maybe I annoyed the gentleman-journalist in charge. I do know that *The Statesman* also has its African and 'black experts' and can only surmise, since the articles dealt with Africa that, in the absence of any explanation whatsoever they were not held up because they were not up to standard. Because an article on the same theme, and not as good as mine I was told by others, was published not long afterwards in *The Statesman*.

It makes me sad to write this letter. I worked in many parts of the world. I successfully fought against and ended the special relationship which existed at one time between the NUJ and the Society of South African Journalists, and prevented the latter from being recognised by the International Federation of Journalists. I did this because of the racism practised by the Society and the South African press as a whole. That is why it gave me such pleasure to become a full member of the NUJ, which is so steeped in non-racialism. But unfortunately I cannot say the same about the media, except for a privileged few.

I have settled here in Britain, married an English girl and hoped in one way or the other to contribute towards bettering race relations in this country, through the only weapon I can effectively use – the pen. But this is not to be. Together with the small number of black journalists who are struggling in this country, I am a sad and disillusioned black man. Journalism in this country seems to be the preserve of whites only. The black journalist is only good enough for the occasional piece of freelance reportage, but alas, not good enough to enjoy the full advantage of staff jobs. I wonder where *The New Statesman* stands on this matter?

Please forgive me for taking your time, but with apologies, it was your article which set me off. All that I can finally say is that I am a disillusioned, nearly disgusted and sadly becoming an angry and bitter black nigger journalist.

> I remain,
> Yours sincerely,
> Lionel Morrison.

My letter caused some consternation to Dick Crossman who seemed on the whole quite eager to help, but was unable to appreciate the various points raised in it.

Those working for the *Statesman*, he said in his 26 February 1971 reply, were mostly occasional contributors, with a tiny staff of literally three or four people.

In view of my letter he hesitated to ask me for reportage of the 'immigrant community', but felt this was something the paper lacked. So that practically he could not think of anything better at that moment than the suggestion that I should do articles on the 'immigrant community'.

In spite of his reply, my attempts at having features published in the *New Statesman* came to naught.

And then on about 20 December 1971, the Liberal peer, Lord (Ted) Willis in a *World at One* talk attacked the lack of black journalists actually employed on the mass media. I wrote to him hoping that the whole issue would be given some more public airing and action. Since the letter was essentially along the same lines as the one written to Dick Crossman, extracts only are reproduced.

Lord Willis
c/o Liberal Party Organisation
7 Exchange Court
London WC2   20th December 1971

Dear Lord Willis,

It was with great relief and indeed pleasure that I listened to you on The World at One the other day on the lack of coloured journalists actually employed on the mass media. The other points you raised about 'coloured' jokes were good but I would like to single out your very pertinent criticism of the lack of coloured journalists in Fleet Street.

Some of us black reporters and writers have been saying the same for quite a time. And in my experience it is not the so-called liberal papers who are prepared to give black journalists a chance. It is papers who in some eyes are not so liberal. They have been less hypocritical. They do not speak of non-racialism in high sounding phrases – they rather act on it more positively than papers who have a so-called liberal tradition.

We are not asking for special favours. Many of us have the ability. What we ask for is just a chance. We are sure we will not upset staff relations, nor will our presence result in any problems.

I am sorry for this letter. But when I heard you over the radio the other day, I thought 'here was a man who knows what it is all about'. Maybe, when you have some time in the future we could meet. I would like to *tell* you all about how we black journalists see things in this country.

With best regards and a Merry Christmas to you,
        Yours sincerely,
                Lionel Morrison.

Needless to say I received no acknowledgement to my letter which was not wholly surprising. I had long learnt that it was easy for people to rave and rant about injustice and racialism and then do little about it practically.

One point needs updating. ITN has subsequently recruited its first black reporter, Trevor MacDonald, who did his ground work in Trinidad before coming to work for the BBC overseas services at the end of the 'sixties. Now his work for ITN is the regular television journalist's diet. He does not get typecast with 'racial' stories and is used as a standard reporter. What is interesting to note is that the very few blacks who have made it on to the nationals or TV have not been trained in Britain, but instead have come here already experienced and prepared to go to work, that is if they can get any.

In *Race and the Press*, published by the Runnymede Trust in 1971, four distinguished journalists – Clement Jones, then editor of the Wolverhampton *Express and Star*; Hugo Young, assistant editor and chief leader writer of the *Sunday Times*; Peter Harland, editor of the Bradford *Telegraph and Argus*; and Harold Evans, editor of the *Sunday Times* – pleaded for special treatment in the press for race relations. They argue their cases eloquently, but, except for Peter Harland, editor of the *Telegraph and Argus* of Bradford, none of them predictably think it of any importance to raise the question of employing 'immigrant' reporters.

Harland, on the other hand, raises the danger of reporting about blacks in crisis situations only and rightly concludes that the impression is soon gained that blacks are problematic.

'What is required is conscious editing, the paper going out to find other kinds of news from among the immigrant community – the same kind of news as the paper prints about the host community, good news as well as bad: meetings, dinners, celebrations, speeches, presentations, retirements, sport and so on.'

And quite rightly he naturally concludes what the others do not, that '*One way of helping towards this end is to employ immigrant reporters* [author's emphasis]. There can be difficulties, arising out of different standards of education, training and qualifications between one country and another, but they are not unsurmountable. And in any case, as immigrant children leave English schools, they should, provided they have the necessary five "O" levels, make suitable candidates for the training scheme operated across the country by the National Council for the Training of Journalists. *It is up to the editors to begin to employ them'* [author's emphasis].

The four contributors to the publication all come to the conclusion as a whole that objectivity in race relations reporting is not achieved without a positive commitment to seek it. This conclusion all editors of British papers would swear they agree with. They might even go so far as to support the need for specialized skills and training in journalism when it comes to this sensitive area of race relations. But how many of them would agree (and act on this agreement) that the training and employment of black journalists would help tremendously to meet this situation? The absence of black journalists in the British press is proof of this hypocrisy which has so befuddled our press to date. A sad epitaph for a country with some of the greatest newspapers in the world.

8. Reporting Race Relations

Derek Humphry

I am often asked how I came to be a race relations reporter. It is a good question, not only because Peter Evans of *The Times* and I are the only ones consistently doing the job in national newspapers, but because the reasons why I came into the job and remain in it help to answer many of the questions about media coverage.

I should make it clear that neither Peter Evans nor I write exclusively about race affairs. He combines his attention to the subject with being Home Affairs Correspondent of his newspaper while I also write about civil liberties, policing, and am on call for 'hard news' reporting when necessary. As yet there is not sufficient need for full-time race relations reporters and it may well be there never will be cause. It would, of course, be possible now for reporters to justify their existence writing solely about race (provided their papers were prepared to allocate the space), but this I think could be unsatisfactory. It might make them stale, working in a relatively narrow field; secondly, working in the broader field of the administration of justice, policing, urban renewal, Home Office policy and so forth keeps the journalist in much broader touch with those affairs which tend anyway to cross-fertilize with race questions.

Lastly, but by no means least, a reporter working 100 per cent on race for a lengthy period would be in danger of over-involvement which might tend to unbalance him. Indications of this danger can be seen amongst some social workers whom I have observed virtually to 'crack-up' after trying to sustain too deep a commitment to black people's problems and finding that the continuing frustrations are eventually beyond their capacity to bear.

I began reporting race relations on the crest of the wave of public interest in the subject created by Enoch Powell's 1968 speeches against the passing of the Race Relations Act. During twenty years of previous reporting I had only occasionally written about immigration or colour problems. My personal involvement only went so far as adopting, in 1957, a boy who, by pure chance so far as my wife and I were concerned, was of mixed race.

Powell brought a libel suit against the *Sunday Times* in 1969 for remarks made about him in a leading article written by the chief leader writer. It would be tempting fate to repeat those remarks now: suffice it to say that the paper decided to defend itself vigorously against the action by pleading 'justification'. This defence requires, when it reaches the courts, much more than astute argument by lawyers – it needs solid evidence to back it up. I was asked to stop writing for the paper and concentrate for so long as necessary on gathering evidence of the effects of Powell's speeches on the black community in Britain.

It proved to be a fascinating and rewarding experience which lasted six months instead of the intended one month. I spent all my time moving from one centre of black population to another, talking to blacks and concerned whites. Almost without exception, people were so anxious to help the *Sunday Times* defend itself against Powell that the cooperation I received was quite remarkable. In gathering the evidence for our lawyers I built up a wide general knowledge of immigration and black settlement. Even more important, I made many lasting friendships amongst a variety of black people – lawyers, doctors, businessmen, social and youth workers, bus drivers and militants and many others – who invariably provide me with background advice and information when I need it.

Enoch Powell v. the Sunday Times never came to trial. An announcement was made in the Queen's Bench Division in April 1970 to the effect that both sides had cleared up their differences of opinion over the meaning of two sentences of the leading article. Mr Powell conceded one point and the newspaper conceded another. Under the terms of the settlement Mr Powell paid his own legal costs and no damages were paid by the *Sunday Times*, which took the unusual step of writing another leading article about the libel action immediately it was settled. (Normally it is part of a settlement that neither party shall say more than the agreed statement.)

And so, curiously, it was Powell who started me off writing about race relations. Moreover, much of the material I gained in that six months of journeying went into the Penguin book I wrote in cooperation with Gus John, *Because They're Black*, which won us the 1972 Martin Luther King Memorial Prize for the best book published in Britain or America contributing to racial harmony.

It is common knowledge that from 1968 onwards race became a subject to which the news media had to pay increasing attention. Coverage has suffered from two major and related drawbacks: first, the popular papers only give the subject space when it is hot news, rarely, if ever, writing about the events which led up to the riot, controversy or whatever has suddenly brought it into the headlines. Second, from 1969 race has become an important electoral issue and vote-seeking politicians will often turn a minor or long-ignored matter on its head to capture publicity and support at the polling booths.

The 'heavy' papers – *The Times*, the *Guardian*, the *Observer* and the *Sunday Times* – will cover race relations matters on their merits regardless of their newsworthiness *vis-à-vis* the other newspapers, but it has to be said that even these worthies will only devote so much space to the subject. They know that their readers will be interested, either through involvement or compassion, in race stories – but there is a limit. At a certain point they know that they will either bore their readers (it is, after all, their job to sell their newspaper and if they don't the 'message' will not get over) or that a surfeit of one topic will start a reaction. At one stage when the *Sunday Times* was carrying a good many stories about black people there was a

Fleet Street joke going around that 'The only difference between the *Sunday Times* and *Anti-Apartheid News* is the price'.

Each of the serious papers has an unspecified, unwritten quota of liberalism beyond which it is not likely to stray. There are, nevertheless, many earnest attempts at in-depth reporting of the background to issues. That other serious newspaper, the right-wing *Daily Telegraph*, will also devote considerable space to race and immigration but generally on the same yardstick as the popular papers – when the subject has been highlighted by a controversy.

The exceptions to this are when immigrants or black citizens come into the newsman's sights in the role of a malefactor or by some freakish or anti-social behaviour. During 1972 and 1973 the outstanding examples of this were concerned with illegal immigration which, quite apart from the cloak-and-dagger and racketeering aspects, were closely connected with political advantages as the government of Edward Heath strove to appear to his supporters to be firm with the blacks even though it had been obliged to let in 27 000 Ugandan Asian refugees.

Real and imagined landings of Asians provided lots of spicey stories. In some instances, when small groups of men were seen landing in small boats, if they had healthy sun-tans and looked a bit swarthy, the police were called to suspected illegal immigrants. Often these stories got into the papers with the footnote that it was a false alarm with good intent. Such instances provided a few jokey paragraphs under a bright headline. On the other hand, the success of the police in intercepting several groups of real illegal immigrants during the summer of 1973 provided a series of 'splash' stories on such a scale that it seemed Britain was undergoing a sizeable foreign invasion. In reality the numbers involved were a few score.

The reasons why a newspaper will give prominence to a story in which the basic ingredient is colour lie in the professionalism and detachment of the British journalist. In itself a good quality, this tradition of non-involvement nonetheless leads to publicity for events which might be better left alone, or treated differently, if more thought and care were applied. The British journalist is taught to be fair, accurate and take care to give both viewpoints an airing. This, some feel, absolves them from thinking any further. They feel this standard enables them to publish any story, no matter how controversial, because their account will be 'balanced' and therefore no intelligent person can take offence. Of course, no rational person can, but such people are not the majority of readers of the press. I have asked journalists on other papers why they played such-and-such a story the way they did, pointing out the consequences in human terms, and invariably the reply is: 'We just reported the facts. Blacks are news. It was fair game.' An example of this was in 1971 when a Pakistani doctor working in the casualty department of a London hospital decided he was unable to successfully perform a tracheotomy operation on an eight-month-old girl with a dummy stuck in her throat. It was the lead story in the *Daily Express* under the headline: 'Doctor: I was afraid to operate.' It got similar prominence in the *Daily Telegraph*: 'Pakistan doctor "afraid to try" saving baby.'

The doctor had decided to send the baby to another hospital where he thought she would receive the best surgical treatment but the child died en route. The *Telegraph*'s medical consultant added a footnote to the inquest report saying that 'a tracheotomy should be within the competence of every practitioner'. It is apparently nearer the truth to say that this operation is very dangerous, especially on a baby, and since the elimination of diphtheria only specialists are taught how to perform it. The effects of the publicity caused the doctor to resign his position.

Some editors pontificate about their liberal sentiments on race, and how careful they are not to offend or to stir up trouble. Doubtless they are well-meaning. But the reality of newspaper life is that their staff generally have the last word about what goes into the paper because the editor cannot be present at the sub-editor's desk all the time to take nuts-and-bolts decisions. If the journalist allocating stories to the columns is either racist or a 'fair game' man then there is little the editor can do about it on most occasions. There are just as many racist journalists as there are racist policemen and racist politicians and it ill behoves the leader writers to call for more coloured policemen in order to influence the attitudes of the police services while there are virtually no black journalists, either within the national news media or (and this is the most tragic) being trained in the provincial press.

What few black journalists there are quite naturally feel drawn to working for the immigrant newspapers which need their multi-lingual talents. Most are comparatively recent residents in Britain and would find it hard to compete with indigenous journalists in a profession where a myriad of subtleties and complexities must be understood in order to write widely understandable (and legally safe) articles. Black journalists are not coming to Fleet Street from the provincial training grounds, nor do they seem likely to in the immediate future, not necessarily because of job discrimination, but for reasons of educational qualification.

A minimum of five 'O' levels, including English, are required before a teenager may join the training scheme of a local newspaper. Not many black youngsters, as a percentage of those passing through the schools, are reaching that level of attainment at the moment and those who do, for good reasons, choose to take other jobs. There are West Indian youngsters who would dearly love to be journalists, yet with all the educational problems which beset their transference from the Caribbean to Britain have little hope of reaching the required standard.

The newspaper unions and managements will not relax their recruiting standards any more than will the teaching profession which refuses to take New Commonwealth teachers until they have undergone a two-year course. Inevitably it will be some years before blacks can be seen in the newsrooms in the same proportion as on the streets. Nevertheless, this could be speeded up if newspapers would make some effort to find suitable recruits and then sponsor them while they get the necessary educational qualifications. Until there is a sprinkling of black journalists on British newspapers the intolerance and thoughtlessness in some newspaper production will continue, and the black community will continue to feel aggrieved that the national news media is exclusively white-dominated and does not understand nor sympathize with their problems. Where there is no sympathy with a subject there is scant coverage.

Many journalists fall into the same trap as the police in equating Black Power with violence, revolution, a take-over … or something. The term has a glamourous aura about it which is heaven-sent to working journalists who depend so much on 'shorthand terms' in order to help convey to readers in the space of a few words the substance of some quite complicated matter. Other examples of shorthand terms in connection with the reporting of race are 'powellism', 'white liberal' and 'do-gooder'. Generally the terms are thought up on the spur of the moment according to the flavour of the story. In a curious way the title of the government's agency to combat discrimination, the Race Relations Board, appeals to journalists because it seems to embrace everything about the problem. Frequently journalists refer to the Race Relations Board when they mean the Community Relations Commission. Neither of these two organizations was, as it turned out, well-named either for the media's or the public's purposes, resulting in confusion of roles, but that would have been difficult to forecast at the time they were set up. If ever they should merge, as has been canvassed, a top priority should be the re-naming of the organization, for race relations is all about public attitudes and responses.

Newspaper policies and practices on whether it should be stated in an article that the person was coloured is yet another area where there is unevenness of application or no policy at all.

To take as an example the case reported in the *Sunday Telegraph* (17.10.71) of a woman found dead in her house. 'The police said they wanted to interview a coloured man who was believed to have been living in the house', said the last of the three paragraphs. The reader was not told whether the woman was black or white, although there was an implication that she was reasonably well-to-do because the value of her house was said to be £17 000.

In contrast, the same day's *Sunday Express* reported the killing in thirteen paragraphs and said that a man who had been staying at the house was sought to help in inquiries. The report made no reference to colour.

The *Sunday Express* is not exactly the immigrant's friend, but in this case acted, in my view, commendably. It seemed apparent from both reports that the killing was not racial, and it may not have been the coloured man responsible anyway. Here was a case where the man's ethnic origin should have been excluded. Of course, the *Sunday Telegraph* might argue that the man's race was part of his description and as he was being sought they were justified in stating it. It is a thorny problem and the only way to tackle it is to have a policy of not stating the man's colour unless, after due consideration between senior journalists, it is considered necessary to do so.

Where the incident reported is clearly involved with racial problems then there should be no pussy-footing about. We have not yet achieved a multiracial society and it does not help towards achieving that end by fudging the true facts.

Another dangerous trap for journalists is too rapid judgement of whether the incident to be reported is racial. The classic example of this was the firebombing of houses in Bradford in 1971 when several newspapers and magazines assumed that the culprits were whites with fascist tendencies, on the grounds that every home attacked was that of an Asian immigrant. It turned out to be more of a tribal feud and eventually other Asians were convicted of the offences. It was a tragic case of journalists – and some commentators – jumping to what seemed obvious conclusions because of the amount of antagonism against Asians which, around that time especially, was being expressed by extreme right-wingers.

The Press Council was asked to adjudicate in a complaint against the *Daily Mirror* over the Bradford fires and found that 'a newspaper has responsibility to take particular care in circumstances fraught with political, racial and social implications. The Council considers the *Daily Mirror* acted irresponsibly in making a serious assumption which the facts did not justify. The complaint is upheld.'

It is not easy for considered judgements always to be made on daily newspapers, morning and evening, sending out editions hourly. It is comparatively simple for papers like the *Sunday Times* to make an investigation and come up, after several days or perhaps even weeks, with an article much nearer the truth. A handicap for the daily papers is that often they lack a reporter who, from rapid inquiries among his contacts, could provide a few instant facts from which his superiors could make deductions.

Because the reporting of race relations requires a good general knowledge of immigration history, law and policy, something which can only be acquired over a considerable period of time due to its complexity, reporters who take an interest in race matters often wish to pass on to other fields before they can really contribute something to the subject. It is relevant that Peter Evans of *The Times* and myself are both in our forties, and find reporting race relations (together with the Home Affairs and civil liberties fields) interesting and absorbing. Speaking for myself, I am not necessarily looking for the promotion or fame as an overseas correspondent which is the justifiable aim of many younger journalists. Here again, the news media cannot criticize the police for not keeping men working on community relations for longer than a year when they do not do so with their own staffs. The stage must soon be reached when national papers and broadcasting channels appoint a race relations reporter on a permanent basis (even if part time) just as they would appoint a political or agricultural correspondent. The intricacy and sensitivity of the subject requires special handling which only the expert can attempt to provide.

The *Guardian* gives more news column space to reporting

and the *Sunday Times* to background investigation and information of race than do any other papers. The reasons for the *Guardian*'s interests in the subject are not precisely known to me, but from reading the paper and knowing many of their staff the apparent answer is a keen social awareness. The motivation of my own newspaper is explained by what I consider to be its general purpose in British journalism: to investigate, explain and comment upon those issues which other newspapers, by reasons of time shortage, finance or default, do not adequately cover.

Another crucial factor is that Harold Evans, the editor of the *Sunday Times*, counts race relations amongst his priority subjects. Following his various pronouncements and talks on the subject he has become something of the oracle as to what should be reported and how; albeit an oracle more respected outside of the profession than within it. Both Harry Evans and Michael Randall, the senior managing editor, demonstrated their commitment to the issue in the middle 1960s when they served on the Archbishop of Canterbury's National Council for Commonwealth Immigrants which became the Community Relations Commission with the passing of the 1968 Race Relations Act. Randall left the Council disillusioned at Labour's passing of the 1968 Commonwealth Immigrants Act (which kept out the East African Asians) and Evans because of a desire not to be part of what is now a government sub-department, which would conflict with his role as a campaigning journalist.

This commitment at the top of management has enabled me to spend considerable time on race relations, resulting in compassionate and critical handling of my articles and, where deserved, a generous allocation of news space. Much of what I have not had printed in the *Sunday Times,* either through shortage of space or disagreement as to its value to the paper's readership, has gone into my three books on race relations with the full approval of the editorial management.

Generally speaking this sympathy with writing about race filters right down through the staff, but certainly no more so than writing about other subjects such as poverty, homelessness, thalidomide babies, crippled persons and so forth. This concern is a measure of the quality of the staff (numbering around 120) of what I consider to be one of the world's great newspapers which is, nevertheless, not without its faults and drawbacks.

The key to reporting race relations for the individual reporter is how (assuming he or she is white and English as I am) to get on with black people. It is comparatively easy to have a drink with a black in a pub, or work next to him on the factory shop floor, but another thing to interview him, perhaps at a time of personal crisis, and then put an account of his problem or whatever into a white, capitalist newspaper towards which he may well be hostile.

At first meeting between the white reporter and black person there is the crisis of confidence. The black is probably asking himself: 'Is this journalist my enemy? What does his paper really want? Am I going to be able to explain myself properly, given linguistic problems and different life styles?' The reporter is wondering what the black person is wondering so that he can make the correct remark to soothe these fears. Usually there is a preliminary sparring session which is useful while each tunes in to the other accent, dialect and motivation for meeting.

Reporting black people, whether from the Caribbean, Africa or Asia is very much a matter of practice in order to learn what they mean by their brand of English. One learns which areas they are prone to exaggerate, which they feel most deeply about, and – most important for a journalist – where they might be pulling one's leg. I could not really begin to write a guide on white-to-black communication; it is so much a matter of touch. Of course, apart from a few journalists, this skill is also picked up by good social workers, probation officers, solicitors and the like.

West Indians are fond of banter and argument and never spare me. Often as I turn up at a conference there are shouts of 'Here's the white liberal press', and asides like 'You're a good white liberal, Derek'. It is important, I found at the outset, to stand up to blacks in an argument and slug it out verbally. They respect a person who will 'have it out' with them on a fair and equal basis; they despise sentimental white racial guilt. An understanding of British colonial history, on which black people inevitably base their historical political thinking, is a basic essential to race relations reporters.

9. Race Today, Gone Tomorrow

Alexander Kirby

If you want to remove inequality, you won't do it by giving equal treatment to unequally placed groups or individuals. Only *unequal* treatment, designed to remove special disabilities, holds out any hope of ultimately achieving equality. This doctrine of positive discrimination lay behind the introduction of the Race Relations Acts of 1965 and 1968, however weakly it has been translated into practice in them: the Acts exist, not to confer special privileges, but to remove the special disabilities which black people suffer through discrimination. Yet it is profoundly depressing that many of those who give whole-hearted assent to the *idea* of positive discrimination recoil in horror when they are faced with it working in practice. This, essentially, was the reason why *Race Today* nearly ceased to be. And the fight over *Race Today* illustrates many of the contradictions inherent in the race relations business, and in press reporting of race.

At the time of the events described in this chapter *Race Today* was the monthly magazine of the Institute of Race Relations (it is now published by an associated body, Towards Racial Justice, which is legally and financially separate from the Institute). The Institute itself was founded in 1958, and was the first independent (i.e., non-governmental) body in Britain concerned with race relations. During its first few years it was concerned primarily with race relations in Central and Southern Africa, and it was only in the mid-sixties that its main research effort began to focus on Britain, in the light of the entry of large numbers of black Commonwealth citizens to the country. Research was the *raison d'être* of the Institute, and the research findings were published in its books and journals. Additionally, it boasted a unique library and information service. It had a monthly newsletter, which was essentially a small circulation house magazine until it was transformed in May 1969 into *Race Today*, an illustrated glossy which was intended to reach a much wider audience.

Race Today's birth predated by two months the publication of the crowning achievement of the Institute's research, *Colour and Citizenship*. This was a massive report on race relations in Britain, summarizing the findings of the Institute's Survey of Race Relations in Britain, begun five years earlier. In quantitative and demographic terms, certainly, it *was* the Institute's crowning achievement: but there were voices to be heard saying that *Colour and Citizenship* was very short on critical analysis of the British situation, and that its 700 odd pages of recommendations added up to a largely uncritical pat on the back for the policies of the Labour Government then in power.

Any enterprise with the scope and aims of the Survey must expect criticism, but what really began to spell out the tensions within the Institute itself was criticism from within. In January 1971 Robin Jenkins, a researcher at the Institute, gave an address to a private meeting of a section of the British Sociological Association in which he criticized *Colour and Citizenship* essentially for not declaring – or even recognizing – its own philosophical framework and ideological position, which he, too, defined as one of support for Labour policies.

The principal author of *Colour and Citizenship*, Jim Rose, had been co-opted to membership of the Institute's Council, its governing body, after the book's publication, and he pressed for Jenkins' dismissal from the staff for criticizing the work of colleagues (several of those who had worked on the Survey and *Colour and Citizenship* were still members of the Institute's staff) in this way. Most of the Institute staff thought that Jenkins' criticisms were valid, and that he had not only a right but a duty to express them. Jenkins eventually resigned six months later, but by then positions had hardened, and there was a clear gap between those (most of the Council) who believed that detached academic work in the traditional mould

G

was all that IRR could and should undertake, and the greater part of the staff, who maintained that such academic work was valid only when coupled with something more immediate and responsive to the realities of racism. The argument spilled over into the ordinary membership of the Institute (about 300 people with some interest in race relations – journalists, academics, social workers and the like) and the annual general meeting in the summer of 1971 saw the first contested election of Council members in the Institute's history. Lord Walston, the Labour life peer who had been a junior government minister and was the Institute's chairman, lost his place on the Council, and five new members were elected, all of them younger people with greater knowledge of race relations at a day-to-day level.

This was the already contested ground over which the battle for *Race Today* would be fought. By now almost two and a half years old, the magazine had begun to acquire a personality of its own, and one which attracted support from outside the Institute and opposition from the Council. I had been editing it for eighteen months, and had always seen it as a vehicle of journalistic positive discrimination: it seemed to me that its great potential lay in opening its pages to the expression of views by people who were on the receiving end of racism – the voice of the victims themselves. This I saw as its unique contribution, to be tackled together with the publishing of research and the provision of a forum for discussion of policies by workers such as community relations officers and others directly involved with race relations agencies.

Race Today was at the time (as it continued to be until after the battle had been fought and won) a thirty-six page monthly, produced by a secretary and myself, with the Institute's information officer writing the four-page Area Round-Up section every month. That scale of operation leaves little time for promotion, yet one of the Council's constant criticisms was that sales did not rise fast enough and that *Race Today* lost money (in fact it cost about one-eighth of the Institute's annual expenditure). But other complaints began to be heard more and more often: that *Race Today* contained too little 'fact' and too much 'opinion', and that it lacked balance. To these I have only this to say: that subjective views sincerely held are, for those concerned with human beings rather than sociological data, an objective fact which we cannot afford to ignore, and that I have never seen it as part of my job to inject an arbitrary and artificial element of balance into my reporting of a grossly unbalanced reality. There is no balance discernible to a workless, homeless black youth in Brixton or Moss Side: to him the scales appear weighted down immovably against him. So who are we to soften the edge of his anguish with our 'balanced' presentation? As Bernard Coard wrote to the Institute in a letter of support at the height of the crisis: 'Academic research which uses terminology to obscure or soften reality performs a disservice to people in desperate circumstances. . . .' There is no balance in our racially discriminatory immigration laws, nor any honest purpose in pretending that there is. It is worth noting that the Institute's amassing and presentation of 'balanced', researched facts about black people had been accompanied, since the passing of the first Commonwealth Immigration Act in 1962, by a progressive worsening of race relations in Britain, by an ever more precipitate flight by whichever government was in power towards the mindless politics of prejudice. It seemed to all of us involved with *Race Today* (which meant virtually the whole Institute staff, not simply those of us who worked on the magazine full-time) that another, more direct approach was needed if people were to be enabled to know how deep the corrosion of racism was biting, something which the Institute's traditional approach could not – on its own – hope to tell them. And if that meant that *Race Today* lacked 'balance', then we would question not our presentation but the motives of those to whom balance was so important. The comments of an ex-conciliation officer of the Race Relations Board, in an article he wrote for *Race Today* before its future was assured, are pertinent here, although the piece was not published until May 1972. The officer, Arthur McHugh, was discussing the opposing factions in the Institute (and other sections of the race relations 'industry') and asked rhetorically whether the truth did not lie 'somewhere between "prejudiced reaction" and "irresponsible extremism" . . .? Regretfully, I find it impossible to conclude this piece on such a balanced note, for the simple reason that it would be at odds with what I saw and heard and learned for myself. What I found was that black people in this country are insulted day in and day out, in the normal course of social relationships; that they are often cheated of jobs and houses without even being aware of the fact; that racist ideas are being perpetuated in schools by racist educationists; and that there is a special, inferior brand of justice for the black citizen. I found widespread disillusion with the bumbling little race relations committees that potter about in the best tradition of colonial paternalism; and an equally widespread conviction among black people that [the Community Relations Commission and the Race Relations Board] lacked both the imagination to grasp their problems, and the power to deal with them. I also discovered that if you say these things out loud, you're a dead duck.'

To ask Council members just what it was in *Race Today* that they disliked specifically almost always brought a reply whose vagueness made it impossible to counter: one of the most frequent of these umbrella criticisms, for instance, was that *Race Today*'s 'style and tone' were at fault. But certain issues of the magazine did arouse specific antagonisms, and fairly definitely expressed ones, which would be communicated to us by some means or another. The first number which we learnt had fluttered the dovecotes in this way was the issue for July 1970, in which John Reddaway, the senior administrative officer of the Community Relations Commission for just over a year until his resignation at the end of 1969, wrote a piece which we entitled: 'Whatever Happened to the Community Relations Commission?' His thesis was summed up in one sentence: 'The real explanation of the Commission's failure to make its mark is . . . simply that it has not so far managed to equip itself with administrative machinery capable of discharging its functions with tolerable efficiency'. Even the muted and informed criticism of an ex-senior employee of unimpeachable antecedents (Mr Reddaway had been Deputy Commissioner-General of the UN Relief and Works Agency and held both the CMG and the OBE) was held to be out of place in an Institute publication.

The following January we published 'Letter from Prison', an account of life in Strangeways Jail, Manchester, written by a black man then serving a year's sentence there. The article was brought out of the prison specifically for publication in *Race Today*.

February saw an article by Peter Hain, following on the success of the Stop the Seventy Tour campaign in getting the South Africans' cricket tour cancelled. His article contained these two sentences: 'British support for apartheid through economic investment is so entrenched and so unprincipled that it is very unlikely that it will be undermined unless we are prepared to mount serious and effective, rather than symbolic, action. Businessmen do not talk in morals: we must be prepared to challenge them on their own territory.' Shortly after it was published an official of the Standard Bank, one of IRR's supporters, telephoned Professor Hugh Tinker, director of the Institute, to say that publication in *Race Today* of further articles by Hain would result in the Institute having few corporate subscribers left.

The March *Race Today* was devoted almost entirely to criticism of the new Immigration Bill. *Race Today* said nothing in favour of the Bill because we believed there was precisely nothing to be said in its favour: it was, as the editorial pointed out, 'not so much an Immigration Bill, more a way of keeping the Tory backwoods quiet'. Yet there was criticism from the Council (as usual, vague and indirect) on the grounds that *Race Today*'s coverage should have achieved 'balance' by finding something positive to say about the Bill.

After that we had a fairly clear run till the autumn, apart from an article entitled 'The "Contradictions" of Black Power', by Obi Egbuna, which was published in the August and September issues. Obi had attracted attention, not only as a playwright, but also as a so-called Black Power leader, and we were not surprised that his piece gave rise to the odd low growl from the Council. But October really did send the balloon up.

That month we published four pieces on the interpretation by the Race Relations Board of the two Acts of Parliament which it had been set up to implement. It was pure chance that the four pieces appeared together, but as they were all offered to me at roughly the same time I decided that they would have greater impact published together than if I were to spread them over several months. The four were a think piece by a Bow Group researcher, an open letter to the Board's chairman from a dissatisfied complainant, a retrospective piece by an ex-conciliation officer (who had left the Board's service eighteen months earlier), and an article by a serving conciliation officer, Tim Hetherington, who was on the point of leaving the Board. Hetherington had, in fact, submitted his resignation, but the Board refused to accept it as soon as it learnt that his article was about to appear in *Race Today*. Instead, Hetherington was suspended and finally dismissed, with the Board later obtaining an injunction restraining him from entering its premises or disclosing confidential information.

The essence of Hetherington's article was a two-fold criticism of the Board's operations, based on several years' first-hand experience of them: he claimed that it took a very long time to decide complaints submitted to it (twenty months in one case he cited), and that it bent over backwards to accept any excuse from alleged discriminators. He gave as an example the case of an Indian who had not even been called for interview for a clerical job with the Inland Revenue, who explained this to the Board on two grounds: there was, they said, an age limit of forty for the job (the applicant was thirty-eight), and their interviewing officer did not have time to decide whether the applicant's two MAs and his law degree from Lucknow University were the equivalent of the five 'O' levels needed to do the job. Furnished with this information, the Board formed the opinion that no unlawful discrimination had occurred. And Hetherington concluded: 'At the moment the Board appears to have little or no coherent strategy and seems incapable of positive action. As it lurches from one internal crisis to another, next to nothing is achieved for all the public money spent. Far from furthering the cause of racial equality, I believe, the Board is doing no more than act as an official buffer to any real expression of black people's rights. I think the time has come for a public reassessment of the Board's role and the way it is operating the Race Relations Act.'

The Board was highly critical of me for neither giving it the chance of rebutting Hetherington's criticisms *in the same issue* of *Race Today* as the one in which they appeared, nor telling it that Hetherington's article was to appear at all, although I did offer it space in the next issue. I had good reason for concealing publication of the piece till the last possible minute, as I believed that the Board, if it knew in advance, would do all in its power to prevent publication. Several years earlier, in fact, there had been a case when an article critical of the Board was removed from the next day's *Sunday Times* on a Saturday afternoon, when the paper was at page proof stage, after consultation between its editor and the Board's chairman. That was why Hetherington and I decided to let the *Observer*, not the *Sunday Times*, have a proof of the *Race Today* piece, timed to appear five days before we published: we thought, correctly as it turned out, that the *Observer* was far enough removed from involvement on a personal level with the captains of the race industry to resist attempts to have the story spiked. But it was a close-run thing, and for an hour or two on the Saturday afternoon we thought the *Observer* might give way. It was largely thanks to the determination of Peter Wilby, the reporter who handled the story from their end, that it did, in fact, make next morning's front page.

It seemed better, therefore, to let the Board fulminate about my allegedly unprofessional conduct as a journalist than to let it succeed in smothering Hetherington's story, as we were convinced that publication was incontrovertibly in the public interest. With its personal contacts with many of the IRR Council members, the Board would have had little difficulty in having the story dropped.

Probably that October 1971 issue made the subsequent fight over *Race Today* inevitable, given the Council's own

entrenched position and our refusal to tell less of the truth
as we perceived it. After that attack on one of the race industry's sacred cows there could be no compromise. But still
there were several months left during which, in Tinker's
phrase, the Council was prepared 'to wound, but not to
strike'. Surprisingly little notice was taken by most Council
members of an avowedly Marxist article in the November
issue by Marios Nikolinakos on the economics of discrimination. But those who did question its appearance in *Race
Today* had been uncritical of the magazine's publication,
almost a year before, of a Monday Club piece calling for
compulsory repatriation of black people (I now think I
was wrong to have published the repatriation article, no
matter how heavy the internal pressures on me to display
'balance'). Anyway, the Monday Club piece drew not a
whisper from any Council member, to my knowledge.

The issue of *Race Today* for February 1972 was the
detonator of the explosion which two months later was to
split the Institute. There were, first, five separate items on the
police, all of them critical (one of these appeared in Area
Round-Up and so was in no way an expression of editorial
opinion, but simply a digest of a press report). One Council
member felt that balance required at least some compli-
mentary reportage of police activity. The chairman, Michael
Caine, was incensed at an explanatory paragraph I had written,
which read: 'The Community Relations Commission has
decided to discontinue the regular half-page it has contributed
to *Race Today* since 1970, but will continue to supply copy on
matters of interest. The Race Relations Board is taking up our
offer of space, and we hope to carry regular features on
aspects of its work.' This, he said, showed an eagerness to
irritate. I had, in fact, written it conscious of the fact that there
was a readiness on the part of many Council members to be
irritated at *Race Today*, and had sought to provide necessary
information in the blandest possible form. But what united
most Council members in their condemnation of *Race Today*
was that issue's front and back covers. The front showed Lord
Goodman, together with a quotation from the speech he had

made in the House of Lords on 1 December 1971, in support of the Rhodesian settlement terms he had helped to negotiate: '. . . this settlement is the best we were able to achieve . . . Right or wrong, we should seize the opportunity', and a banner headline of my own invention: 'Five million Africans say NO'. This I thought straightforward and factual. It did not protect *Race Today*, however, from later accusations of anti-Semitism. The back cover was simply an advertisement for a demonstration to be organized against the settlement terms by the Anti-Apartheid movement.

One Council member, Lord Seebohm, claimed that the two covers together had lost the Institute between ten and twenty thousand pounds in withheld donations. (It was then approaching the climax of an appeal for £450 000.) Most of those present at the February Council meeting roundly condemned the covers. Normally the Council met quarterly, but after that events moved fast, and an emergency Council meeting was summoned for 20 March.

Before seeing what happened then and in the month that followed, it is worth looking in slightly greater detail at the composition of the Council. The personalities, the good or ill will of the members, are immaterial, and their integrity is not at issue here. What is important to an understanding of events at IRR is a knowledge of the interests represented by Council members, and these were mainly three: the City, academic life, and the race relations business. First, the City members: these were Michael Caine, a director of Booker McConnell, Lord Seebohm (deputy chairman of Barclays Bank), David Sieff (Marks and Spencer), Harry Oppenheimer (Anglo-American Corporation of South Africa Ltd.), Richard Hornby, Conservative MP for Tonbridge (Lexington International Ltd.), Sir Ronald Prain (Roan Selection Trust), and W. G. Runciman (Walter Runciman & Co. Ltd.). Academics included Sir Robert Birley, one-time headmaster of Eton, now at the City University; Lord Boyle, Vice-Chancellor of Leeds University; and Professor Roland Oliver of the School of Oriental and African Studies at London University. Members active in race relations organizations (apart from

G*

some of those already mentioned) included Mark Bonham-Carter (chairman of the Community Relations Commission, and of the Race Relations Board before that), Anthony Lester (Society of Labour Lawyers, and a principal architect of the 1968 Race Relations Act), Joan Lestor, Labour MP for Eton and Slough, Dipak Nandy, Director of the Runnymede Trust, and Jim Rose. All those listed here (except Mr Oppenheimer, who was absent) voted with the chairman on 20 March.

All of them liberals, they believed that, if the Institute were to survive, boats must not be rocked nor toes trodden upon. Only thus could money be raised. So *Race Today* must either be silent, or else be silenced. This left unanswered the questions: 'What sort of Institute? What will it do? And can it do it without *Race Today*?' Two members, admittedly, Joan Lestor and Dipak Nandy, did call for *Race Today* to be more rather than less radical – but they sounded their clarion call only *after* they had voted with the majority at the 20 March meeting. The City members were not willing to go on seeing their colleagues – and sometimes themselves – criticized in *Race Today*'s pages for connivance in exploitation, at home or abroad. The academics feared for the Institute's detachment so long as *Race Today* showed itself keen to become ever more involved (note that we did not seek to halt the Institute's academic work, but only to combine with it an approach which we believed to be both complementary and vital). And the captains of the race industry would not brook further criticism of their own empires.

Several Council members came under more than one of these admittedly fairly arbitrary definitions. And most of them were decent, honourable people. But, given their belief that the Institute must survive at almost any cost, collision was inevitable between them and a staff which was convinced that the only Institute with a moral claim to existence was one which enabled black people to understand their exploiters, not one which helped industry to gain the maximum advantage from each of its production units, no matter what his colour or his culture.

Lest I have given the impression that *Race Today* by now

had a mass black readership, I should make it quite clear that it hadn't. It had no mass readership at all. Throughout its life its circulation has grown every month, but as it started out by inheriting a readership of about 800 from the old IRR newsletter, it had a lot of leeway to make up. At the time of the crisis, by spring 1972, we were selling about 3000 copies a month. And apart from this modest start, and its totally unrealistic staffing, *Race Today* had also to contend with the suspicions of many potential readers who were cool towards anything that emanated from the prestigious IRR. To the extent that it overcame these suspicions it succeeded, for the staff, in becoming the outward and visible sign of the Institute's commitment and willingness to become involved instead of detached. But it was a contradiction never entirely overcome: there were, understandably, black people who were quite prepared to accept Robin Jenkins' advice in his BSA talk and tell the Institute's would-be researchers – and journalists – to 'fuck off'.

The Council members, of course, were able to make play with this pathetically small readership. When we pointed out to them that *Race Today* was written without the deference due to their sensibilities because it was seeking to reach people with a wholly different set of mental furniture – people who were both poor and black – they were able to rejoin that we had very few black readers, or white ones either. To some degree it's the old chicken-and-egg argument: do your readers determine your material, or *vice versa*? All we could do, finally, was to go on in the light of the comments we got from people we knew, black and white. And the sort of rule of thumb we developed said, simply if crudely, that *Race Today* *was* valued by people who were involved in race relations from day to day, either as a profession or because they were black. The examples I have mentioned earlier give some idea of the ways in which we tried to let black people speak for themselves and the extent to which we were willing to be critical of other race agencies (two tasks which went hand in hand: it is impossible to say which damned us further in Council eyes). It is helpful to see some of the unsolicited comments made by a wide range of people, and published in *Race Today* in April and May 1972, once the threat of *Race Today*'s closure was out in the open.

Hal Austin, West Indian freelance journalist and broadcaster, wrote: 'The closure of *Race Today* is regarded by black people as yet another facet of the arrogance and trickery behind the race industry. This closure is another blatant example of the white, middle-class, all-British habit of closing your eyes and pretending that nobody is there. Apart from the trendy "alternative Press", which like its Fleet Street counterparts, has never seen fit to employ black journalists, *Race Today* made it a matter of policy to allow black writers to put their side of the story. It was one of the few – very, very few – journals that dared speak out in the strongest possible terms against the humiliation and brutality that is part of the black experience. . . .' A conference of community relations officers and their assistants passed the following resolution: 'This Conference . . . strongly deplores the decision taken by the Council of the Institute of Race Relations to cease publication of *Race Today* in its present form in the very near future, and it urges the Extraordinary General Meeting when it meets to reverse this regrettable decision'. The General Secretary of the National Union of Journalists, Ken Morgan, issued a press statement which included the comment: 'The decision to close the magazine without any meaningful consultation with its staff or their union is deplorable. Apart from our criticism of it as a piece of bad industrial relations, the NUJ deplores the loss of any magazine dedicated to promoting understanding between races and fighting against racial discrimination.' The children's librarian of the London borough of Lambeth wrote in saying: 'In the course of my work as a librarian in this multiracial borough I find [*Race Today*] invaluable. How else can a busy layman so easily keep in touch with facts and opinions about all aspects of race relations? To me it is as much obligatory reading as *New Society* or *The Times Educational Supplement*, and if it is abandoned, I shall feel as much deprived as if either of them ceased to exist.' The secretary of the Association of Community Relations Officers wrote that *Race Today* had 'established itself over the past eighteen months as the most important single publication for the advance of understanding and the promotion of a just society within the continuance of improved community relations'. Jennifer Hurstfield, a lecturer in sociology at the University of Leicester, commented: '. . . I should have thought that the publication of a popular, non-sectarian journal which discussed, among other things, the political dimensions of race would now be receiving the Institute's highest priority. Instead I learn that *Race Today* is to be summarily shelved. . . .' And the Revd Robert Nind, parish priest of Brixton, had this to say: 'I have worked in Jamaica, from 1960–67, in areas largely supported by emigrants to England. Since 1967 I have worked in Battersea and Brixton, and am closely involved with the black population in their various community problems. Your intention to close down *Race Today* is like a stab in the back. Those whom I have counted friends are, in fact, on the other side. Here has been an intelligent forum for the non-academics to express their views as well as the trained researchers and sociologists, and presented in a way that people will read. . . .' Apart from the letters sent to us there were many letters about *Race Today* and the Institute published in the *Guardian* and *The Times*, one of them claiming that *Race Today* had achieved 'something unique in the history of British journalism'. The Council might be forgiven for thinking that it was on the point of reaping the whirlwind. Certainly none of them can have anticipated that their plans would have aroused such passionate and widespread opposition.

From our point of view this upsurge of support, coming just when we needed it most, was a tremendous boost, similar in kind to encouragement we had received for a considerable time, but far more broadly based. Even so, it could be – and probably was, by some – dismissed as subjective and therefore worthless. What could less easily be argued away was the findings of a survey carried out by an Institute researcher, Malcolm Cross, in April 1972. Admittedly something of a rush job, and rather rough and ready in terms of sociological exactitude, it nevertheless gave a useful guide to the opinions of *Race Today* held by two significant groups, community relations officers and leaders of black groups affiliated to the Joint Council for the Welfare of Immigrants (who provided the list of addresses for circulation of the groups). The survey provided sixty-four replies from people working at one or other of these 'grass-roots' levels. In essence it showed that over 90 per cent of respondents thought *Race Today* useful, and 81 per cent were satisfied with its contents. Asked to compare it with other race relations periodicals, and to rank them in terms of usefulness, representation of black view, and contribution to problem solving, the sample consistently placed *Race Today* top, with the publications of the Community Relations Commission, Race Relations Board and Runnymede Trust scoring far below it.

But the survey, and the comments quoted earlier, came after the fateful emergency Council meeting of 20 March. There the chairman announced his proposal that *Race Today* should 'cease publication in its present form' (no new form was ever discussed with me) after the next (i.e., April's) issue, and that Professor Tinker should be sent immediately on six months' leave until his contract expired the following September. Tinker was under fire primarily because he had sided with the staff in their support for Jenkins and then for *Race Today*, and it was a major error on the Council's part to try to tackle both Tinker and *Race Today* together. Had they kept the issues apart, it is quite possible that they would have had far greater success.

Those members of staff present at the meeting (Tinker, the departmental heads, and two of us as elected staff representatives) had had to leave the room while the plan was debated; we were called back in to be told that it had been agreed by all the original Council members save one who voted with the five new members elected the year before. His had always been a lonely voice of reason. On behalf of the staff we all made clear that we could not accept it. And then something unusual took place. The entire staff of the Institute, who had stayed on after work (it was now about 8 p.m.) to learn the result of the meeting, came in uninvited to impress upon the Council their rejection of the moves it had just agreed. (The previous December the staff had passed a resolution supporting *Race Today* as 'an objective expression of the values which they and the Institute hold'.) Nothing anyone could say, however, succeeded in persuading the Council to stay its hand, or to think again, until someone pointed out that such a momentous decision would need to be ratified by an emergency general meeting of the whole Institute membership. This was accordingly fixed for 18 April, and meant that *Race Today* had, in fact, two more issues to run.

It is worth noting here that a *Financial Times* reporter whose article the next morning compared the Institute very unfavourably with its South African namesake, trotting out the hoariest 'Reds-under-the-bed' theory in support of his argument, rang up while the meeting was in progress and asked to speak to Anthony Lester. Since most Council members appeared at the Institute only on the occasion of Council meetings (arranged in advance to take place at quarterly intervals, normally) it was obvious that the reporter knew beforehand of this meeting and it is highly probable that he knew of its subject and likely outcome.

That *Financial Times* piece was the first round in the press battle over *Race Today*. I have already mentioned the coverage of the dispute in the letters columns of the *Guardian* and *The Times*, but there was as well a welter of news coverage: a story as full of news value as a bust-up among the *soi-disant* 'race peacemakers' (as the populars labelled the Institute) was too juicy to miss. Most editorial comment portrayed the struggle as one between decent liberals (the Council) and Black Power-crazy Marxist tearaways (the six dissentients and the staff). But most of the news stories were rather more objective and helped to alert our supporters among the membership to what was really at stake.

Few of us thought the vote on April 18th would go in our favour. But one very ill-judged speech by a member of the Council majority, and some cogent and principled speaking from our supporters, meant that the issues at stake – academic and journalistic freedom and responsibility – were seen to be under threat, and after three hours' wrangling we had won: the meeting passed, by ninety-four votes to eight, a resolution congratulating the director of the Institute and the editor of *Race Today* (and so, by implication, the whole staff) on 'their successful implementation of [the Institute's] basic policy'. The Council majority had already made it clear that they would regard the members' decision as a vote of confidence – or not – in themselves, and so in the next few weeks they all resigned.

Was it a Pyrrhic victory? In the twenty months that have passed since that evening the Institute has had to cut back its activities, make staff redundant, and try desperately to raise funds from sources other than those it had traditionally relied on. Now it looks as if the battle for survival has been lost: there *is* no more money, and, barring a miracle, the Institute has come to the end of the line. (*Race Today* itself is safe for the time being, as *Towards Racial Justice* is separately funded.)

Whether you think the fight before and after April 1972 has been worthwhile must depend on whether you think the Institute of Race Relations ought to exist. If it had accepted the wishes of the Council majority it could have sailed serenely on, cushioned by the money that they would have been able to raise for it, and adding lustre to many an aspiring academic's reputation. Its existence would have been assured – and also, I believe, largely irrelevant. For the strength of the Institute, as of *Race Today* itself, lay in its ability to help the victims of discrimination, prejudice and exploitation to understand what caused their predicament – and by understanding to act. You don't impart that understanding simply through academic research which is aimed at Whitehall, though research will always be one means (among many) to the end. But sometime the amassing of 'facts' has to stop, and calls for more and more facts become not just an irrelevance but a delaying tactic, a means of control. We know all we need to in order to act. What we now have to find is the will.

The Institute's extinction, which now seems almost certain, can achieve more than its continued existence on a false premise ever could. It will show, for a start, that every liberal has his price, and that our famed British tolerance will not tolerate having the mask ripped from its face. Or, as Arthur McHugh put it, 'If you say these things out loud, you're a dead duck'. How many more times does he have to be proved right?

10. Conclusion

Charles Husband

It is not my intention to summarize the contributions which have, in many instances, already been a brief presentation of what could have been much fuller statements. I would only like to point out again the way in which each contribution provided further evidence of the existence of racist bias within the mass media. From different standpoints the authors have stressed the dangerous and unacceptable consequences of such racism and we can be left in no doubt as to the importance of attacking and eradicating this bias. In the introduction I said that the purpose of this book was not to provide definitive answers but to pose unpalatable, but essential, questions. That remains the case and hopefully having invested time and effort in reaching this point each reader will justify this effort by grasping these questions, and particularly the unpleasant ones: To what extent am I unaware of racist assumptions I hold? To what extent do I acquiesce in the continuing media portrayal of racial stereotypes in drama and comedy? To what extent am I dependent upon definitions of events provided by the media? What have I done about countering racism in the mass media? What can I do? – these are questions, some of which are difficult to ask, none of which are easy to answer.

As a beginning I would like to make a few suggestions about practical action which may assist in the process of eradicating racism from the mass media.

The critical significance of the news media has been made apparent in a number of the contributions, and is acknowledged by many respected working journalists: for example,

The attitude of the mass media is a crucial element in race relations. Public opinion on immigration or colour prejudice can be materially affected by the way newspapers, television and radio handle stories concerning them.

P. W. Harland*

It is clear to students of race relations that there is a strong connection between race reporting and racial attitudes among the public; that the newspaper treatment of race relations has an important bearing on the quality of race relations on the ground; hence, that newspapers, when dealing with race, have a peculiarly delicate responsibility.

Hugo Young*

These quotations would reflect the opinion of many journalists, and indeed there is within the National Union of Journalists a group who are actively campaigning to eradicate discrimination in employment and bias in reporting. It would therefore be wrong to assume that journalists are a totally hostile group of unthinking professionals. What we, their audience, can do is to remind them of their social conscience through tactical criticism, precise specification of failings *and* praise for their successes. This would serve at least two functions. For many journalists it would provide welcome feedback on their performance, and secondly these comments would provide visible evidence of the *demand* for improvement which could be used against those in the profession who claim their level of performance is adequate. It is a not infrequent response of media executives when challenged on an aspect of their professional performance to claim that the complainant is in a minority of one, since he cannot remember having heard a similar complaint before. If we, the audience, take our responsibility to comment upon the media more seriously then such a defence should become impossible and those journalists who are working for improvements will be able to point to the existence of external pressure.

Therefore, do not be embarrassed or reticent about voicing complaints or praise. Write to the editor of the paper and

*In *Race and the Press*, Runnymede Trust Publication, 1971.

also, where he is identified, to the particular journalist responsible. Be specific about your objections or praise and where there has been factual error demand that it be corrected, not just apologized for. Should you feel that you have received no satisfactory answer, in the case of the press, you should refer your complaint to the Press Council. This is the body which can adjudicate complaints against a newspaper. It is something of a toothless wonder, being largely financed by the Newspaper Proprietors Association and having no real sanctions it can bring to bear, and yet editors do not enjoy being brought before it. Making complaints to the Press Council can thus be a real pressure upon recalcitrant editors. Also since the current relative absence of complaints is produced as evidence of the good record of the press in reporting race relations, it will help in removing that myth.

In making complaints about the failings of the media, and in registering satisfaction with an aspect of their work, remember that whatever additional leverage you can bring to bear should be deliberately exercised. I remember an example where a complainant was given a page in a local newspaper to rebut a biased account of Jensen's views on race which the paper had printed. The success of this complaint almost certainly resulted from the complainant's use of his minimal professional status in his initial complaint and not from that paper's automatic acceptance of one citizen's comments. If you have any particular status other than Mr or Mrs or Ms Citizen, use it. If you can persuade someone with socially valued status to write in support, then do: JPs; Councillors; MPs; office bearers in trade unions, professional bodies or political organizations are obvious members of the species. Your complaint will carry further weight if it comes from a corporate group. Remember racism and any of its manifestations is 'officially' unacceptable in this society and therefore media staff must tread cautiously when ignoring groups whose concern is the eradication of racism. Thus, for example, the Secretary of the Biddenholm Campaign Against Racism will carry more potential punch than he or his ten fellow members might have when writing as individuals. Particularly is this so when the group is known to be active in ways not confined to letter writing. The local press in particular will have some knowledge of active groups in their area; and yet even here it seems that a small active membership can have a totally disproportionate effect as a pressure group.

When corresponding with editors or other media personnel a scribbled comment on a brutalized piece of notepaper can hardly be expected to help. It is worth the effort to clearly type letters and to carefully draft and revise the content before sending it. Similarly, courtesy in acknowledging replies and commenting on them is a necessary follow-up. Sending off a letter without the intention to follow it up can be an ego-centric piece of self-abuse. Nor should you assume that communication via letter is the only or the best way to register your views. Seeking out a personal meeting with the individual journalist or editor can be much more fruitful. He is likely to be more open and in some ways more vulnerable in that situation. At least normal social politeness makes it difficult for him to avoid your arguments in a way which is all too possible with a letter. If possible it can be very useful to get an editor or journalist to come to speak to your group, whatever its constituency, for statements made in such semi-public settings can be used on later occasions as leverage when the reality of his performance fails to match the promise of his words. And the professional values of journalism make it quite difficult for a journalist in such a group situation to renounce responsibilities which if taken seriously in practice would considerably improve aspects of the reporting of race relations.

Nor should members of the media audience see the creation of news as the monopoly of journalists. Members of the public should take very seriously their own limited powers to generate news. At a basic level you cannot complain if the local press fails to cover a meeting or other event which you have organized if you neglected to give prior notice of its taking place. Give as much advance notice as possible, in writing and keep a copy, and by telephone to the newsdesk. Do not let meetings be ends in themselves; at a minimum agree a press release which, typed and double spaced, you can hand in to the local paper. It is worth keeping a copy of correspondence and press releases which have been sent to a local paper along with cuttings of any news copy which has resulted from it. Some local papers have a distinct bias against anti-racist groups and opinion, and give undue emphasis to negative racial events and to such groups as the National Front. In these cases it is worthwhile comparing the number of column inches you have received compared with such groups; to compare the location in the paper, front page or lost in the inside pages; and to compare the headline sizes. These comparisons can produce 'evidence' which you may put to a local editor and request at least balanced coverage. Obviously in such cases documentation of the efforts you have made to keep the paper informed of your activities is valuable supplementary evidence.

It would be naively optimistic to believe that individuals or groups at a local level can expect guaranteed access to the pages of the local press. It would be equally mistaken to remain passive and see the selection of news as being outside the sphere of influence of ordinary individuals. Strategies such as those outlined immediately above can yield results. Many papers, national and local, have staff who are very sympathetic to anti-racist arguments and it is worth trying to identify these individuals and deliberately feed them information. There are benefits to be had from cultivating such liaisons; which are not without their benefits to the individual journalist. Nor should it be forgotten that many areas are now served by local radio stations, many of whom seem particularly open to ideas for news and current affairs interviews. Regional and national television should not be held in awe. Particularly where you have someone with a national reputation speaking, or where the event is specially topical, or has a specific interest value, the cost of a telephone call is a small outlay. Too much news exists by default, selected from the relative vacuum created by the timidity and passivity of those organizing other potentially newsworthy events. Concern for the reporting of race relations requires the audience to be implicated in the creation of news, nor only commenting upon it after its production.

Of course, a great deal must be accomplished within journalism itself. There already exist codes of practice for reporting race relations which if rigorously applied would go a long way to improving the reporting of race relations, and there exist individual journalists with commitments to eradicating racism who would intelligently implement such a code. What is lacking is a sense of urgency and true concern within the profession as a whole, and particularly is there an absence of continuing editorial leadership. An occasional feature article in no way compensates for routine news stories which reflect a superficial analysis of racial situations and an absence of sensitivity to the reverberations casual reporting of racial issues can have.

There is in essence a need for *positive discrimination* in the reporting of race relations, with the leadership coming from the editors. The lack of credibility which much of the press suffers in black communities, reflected in Wilfred Wood's comments, stems at least in part from the individual journalist's ignorance of the total situation, an aspect of which he is trying to report. The high rate of geographical mobility in pursuit of career advancement can make such ignorance at a local level an occupational hazard. The way to promotion in journalism is often through geographical mobility from one paper to another and such mobility inevitably reduces the possibility of a journalist developing an in depth knowledge of an area, and acceptance within it. The local press in particular need to retain staff who are building contacts within the community for it is the absence of such personal knowledge which leads to journalists using as spokesmen those self-defined leaders who cause so much offence to the black audience. To retain staff will require a new strategy from management and editors which will provide journalists with career and salary incentives and conscious editorial backing. It would be a waste of time cultivating specialist knowledge and awareness in a journalist if his reports are subsequently subjected to the usual sub-editing process of reduction and reorganization by someone lacking that knowledge or concern.

In relation to specific expertise there is at present an obvious need for positive discrimination in the employment of more black journalists. As Lionel Morrison has pointed out the current situation is marked by the extreme difficulty black journalists face in gaining employment. In the current racial climate there *are* issues which black journalists are better equipped to report. And in a different sense there is a definite need for journalists with black consciousness to provide a non-white interpretation of race relations in Britain. The experience of *Race Today* shows how unpalatable such information can be to even the most 'liberal' white sensibilities and thus such journalism would require a formidable degree of editorial courage. But if black journalists are only to be hired, or allow themselves to be hired, to write 'white' news then it would be better if their current near exclusion continued. Positive discrimination in the hiring of black journalists is not meant to merely counter discrimination in employment; it should also be a conscious step toward providing a multi-ethnic perspective on the whole range of newsworthy events and an attack upon the cultural myopia of much of contemporary journalism. Britain is multiracial but her newsmedia still possess a white value system and it is this which black journalists must challenge over the whole range of topics, and not only on those which are visibly 'race' stories.

Throughout journalism there is a need for positive discrimination in the preparation of news stories on racial issues. This would require deliberate questioning of the assumptions underlying party political and popular debate on race. A new honesty in going beyond talk of 'our tolerance' to an analysis of our racist practices and the ways in which we are all implicated in their continuation. A new positive concern to eradicate racism would result in the press not confining itself to exposés of economic exploitation of black labour in southern Africa by multi-national firms, but would make painfully apparent to us all the degree to which we benefit in terms of cheap service industries, cheap hosiery and knitwear, etc, by the exploitation of black labour here in Britain. Positive discrimination in reporting race relations would also require journalists to make use of material which counters those popular myths and stereotypes which, in defining the black population as variously inferior and threatening, help to maintain them as a discriminated minority. Journalism must take seriously its responsibility to analyse and report upon the disease of racism in Britain and cease to merely selectively monitor some of its symptoms.

Quite clearly such innovations require radical changes within journalism. They would challenge head on deeply entrenched news criteria such as negativity, and the imperative of reporting a story on the day it breaks. They would be impossible without a radical rethink of the responsibilities the individual journalist has as author of his material and the time he has available for its preparation. Clearly they require an editorial commitment and willingness to challenge newspaper proprietors which at the present would seem to be an exceedingly scarce commodity.

However, pessimism about the likelihood of success should not be a deterrent to constructive thought and action. A concerted effort which was seen to fail would itself be of value and distinctly preferable to the contemporary amorphous mix of espoused liberalism and concern, which is a mere genuflexion in the direction of this society's official values by senior media personnel, and the isolated frustration of individuals who are actively striving for improvement from a variety of powerless situations.

Much of what has been said in this conclusion regarding the audience's responsibility for the content of newsmedia applies with equal validity to the entertainment media. Since the television networks are locked in a struggle where financial survival and viewing figures are major criteria of success then we must expect them to continue to transmit those programmes with large viewing audiences, despite any racist connotations embedded in them. The dominance of white personnel in the executive and production staff of television programming aids in continuing the alarming insensitivity to racial aspects of programme content, but they are aided in this to a very significant extent by us, the viewing audience. The proportion of people who comment upon television programmes to the broadcasting companies is minute in comparison to the viewing audience for any programme, and yet perhaps because of the absence of feedback the management do, on occasions, seem almost bizarrely sensitive to such comment. A telephone call to the television company immediately after a programme will usually find the telephonist equipped to put you through to someone who will note your comments. A letter to the station and the individual producer care-of the station could be disproportionately influential in their ramifications. Just as with the press you can take complaints to a higher authority, so, too, with television there is the Independent Broadcasting Authority,* for the commercial channels, and the Programmes Complaints Commission,* for the BBC, which are charged with overall responsibility for programme standards. Making known your views to individual producers and to broadcasting companies can be most worthwhile for, unlikely as it may seem, in an inconsistent way they do seem susceptible to audience reaction.

Perhaps too much attention has been directed toward the national media, certainly too little has been said about minority media. In journalism, film, theatre and literature there exists an alternative to the national mass media and these offer an opportunity to each of us to select and support minority productions which reflect our own interests. In the press there are neighbourhood and ethnic-based newspapers which provide an interpretation of events based on different assumptions to those operating in the national press. It is vital that these sources of non-establishment, non-white viewpoints should be supported, if for no other reason than as an act of self-defence against the monotone definitions provided by the national newsmedia.

Amadu Maddy made apparent the difficulties that can be experienced in trying to develop an independent black aesthetic in the theatre. He also made it very clear how important such an endeavour is in the freeing of black people

*Addresses provided at the end of this section.

in Britain from white cultural imperialism. It is also important for us whites to have the shackles of our cultural conceit removed and our complacency challenged. Support for minority art forms is not the prerogative of the minority, but is valid for all, in their own interest.

This collection of contributions has said only a little of what could be said; and of itself amounts to no more than the reader makes of it. Hopefully, if it reminds us, the audience of the mass media, that passivity is not a natural nor inevitable part of being a newspaper reader or television viewer, then it may make us a little more critical and irritable. If we can nurture that reasonable irritation and feed it by critical observation of the mass media, then, perhaps we can spawn an articulate anger which will express itself in action.

Those working within the mass media may reasonably experience those natural defensive responses that follow an attack upon one's professional competence. I would hope that their very professionalism will make them consider most seriously the implications for necessary change which arise from the contributions in this book.

ADDRESSES FOR REGISTERING COMPLAINTS

For Newspapers

(Remember, before going to the Press Council you must first have made your complaint known to the Editor and given him the opportunity to respond to your complaint.)

The Press Council,
81 Farringdon Street,
London EC4A 4BL

For Commercial Television and Radio

Independent Broadcasting Authority,
Complaints Review Board,
70 Brompton Road,
London SW3 1EY

For the BBC Television and Radio

Programmes Complaints Commission,
BBC,
St Andrews House,
40 Broadway,
London SW1H 0BT

The Contributors

Charles Husband is a lecturer at Leicester University School of Social Work. Formerly he was at the Centre for Mass Communication Research and was co-author with Paul Hartmann of *Racism and the Mass Media* (Davis-Poynter 1974).

Reverend Wilfred Wood is vicar of a parish in Catford. With a considerable background in the development of black self-help schemes, he is currently Chairman of the Martin Luther King Foundation and a member of the BBC's Religious Advisory Committee.

Yulisa Amadu Maddy was born in Sierra Leone and has been Head of Drama on Radio Sierra Leone. He is a playwright, author and actor and whilst in Zambia was trainer of the National Dance Troupe. As a playwright and actor he has direct experience of British mass media.

Jennie Laishley is a Social Psychologist by discipline and has worked in the field of race relations and education. She is co-author of the Fabian pamphlet, 'Education for a multi-racial Britain'. Currently she is working on a Human Relations course for secondary school pupils.

John Downing is Head of the Division of Sociology at Thames Polytechnic. He is actively involved in the fight against racism at grassroots level, and has carried out research into the media handling of race relations.

Graham Faulkner whilst at the Centre for Mass Communication Research at Leicester University carried out research into the role of television in the socialization of immigrants in Britain. He is currently concerned with public participation in urban planning.

Lionel Morrison is one of the very few black journalists working in Britain. He is Chairman of the National Union of Journalists Race Relations Sub-Committee, and is currently completing a book on Black Politics in Britain.

Derek Humphry is a staff reporter on the *Sunday Times* with a particular interest in race relations. He is author of *Police Power and Black People*; and co-author, with Michael Ward, of *Passports and Politics*, a study of the 'Ugandan-Asian Problem'. With Gus John he wrote the award-winning book *Because They're Black*.

Alexander Kirby was Editor of *Race Today* during the period of its transition into a politically conscious journal, which set itself the task of honestly reporting the black experience in Britain. In carrying out this aim, many of the assumptions underlying the 'liberal' commitment to racial justice in Britain were exposed.